About the Author

DR. LAURA SCHLESSINGER received her Ph.D. in physiology from Columbia University and holds a post-doctoral certification and license in marriage and family therapy from the University of Southern California. She is the author of nine *New York Times* bestsellers. Her award-winning, internationally syndicated radio program is heard by more than eight million listeners weekly. Her program can also be heard on XM Satellite Radio and the Armed Forces Network, and is streamed and podcast on www.drlaura.com. She lives in Southern California with her husband.

The
Proper Care
and Feeding
of Marriage

The
Proper Care
and Feeding
of Marriage

Dr. Laura Schlessinger

HARPER

NEW YORK · LONDON · TORONTO · SYDNEY

HARPER

A hardcover edition of this book was published in 2007 by HarperCollins Publishers.

THE PROPER CARE AND FEEDING OF MARRIAGE. Copyright © 2007 by Dr. Laura Schlessinger. All rights reserved. Printed in the United States of America. No part of this book may be used or reproduced in any manner whatsoever without written permission except in the case of brief quotations embodied in critical articles and reviews. For information address HarperCollins Publishers, 10 East 53rd Street, New York, NY 10022.

HarperCollins books may be purchased for educational, business, or sales promotional use. For information please write: Special Markets Department, HarperCollins Publishers, 10 East 53rd Street, New York, NY 10022.

FIRST HARPER PAPERBACK PUBLISHED 2008.

The Library of Congress has cataloged the hardcover edition as follows:

Schlessinger, Laura.
    The proper care and feeding of marriage / Laura Schlessinger.—1st ed.
      xii, 222 p. ; 22 cm.
    ISBN: 978-0-06-114284-0
    ISBN-10: 0-06-114284-0
    1. Marriage. 2. Man-woman relationships. 3. Married people. 4. Intimacy (Psychology). I. Title.
HQ503 .S35 2007
646.7/8 22   306.872 22   2007297436

ISBN: 978-0-06-114282-6 (pbk.)

08 09 10 11 12 NMSG/RRD 10 9 8 7 6 5 4 3 2 1

To all who yearn to love and be loved

Contents

Preface

Is there really ever such a thing as a *perfect* marriage? The answer to that question is, "YES." I know you're stunned. Stay with me here: "perfect" doesn't mean that everything goes right, or your way for that matter, or that you're feeling romantically perky all the time. There are just too many unpredictable events, challenges, and tragedies in life for any of us to feel content and satisfied for any prolonged period of time. Yet even in the midst of misery, you can still feel and believe that your marriage is perfect *if* you have the right attitude; and I don't mean that you think *positively*—I do mean that you think *outwardly*. When you do so, married life becomes perfect no matter what difficulties you're going through.

I took a call from Michelle, a seventeen-year-old high school student, which will clarify:

> **Michelle:** Hi, Dr. Laura! It's a pleasure to speak with you. My question is this: this Saturday is my boyfriend's and my senior prom. As it turns out, we have a conflict because it is also his championship lacrosse game at the same time as the dance. He has told me that I could decide which one we should do.

DrL: Really? So what's your decision?

Michelle: Well, personally, I want to go to the prom because it's our senior prom and it's our last dance together, it's meaningful, you know? But it's also his major opportunity because scouts will be at this game for college recruitment. So for him the best choice would be for the game but I want to go to prom . . . selfishly.

DrL: Do you love him?

Michelle: Of course. Yes.

DrL: Do you imagine you're going to marry him? I'm asking you that because I just want to know the depth of your compassion and caring for him.

Michelle: I can see it. I can definitely see it working, but I'm only seventeen. . . . Yes, I care for him a lot.

DrL: Well then, I guess he's going to his lacrosse tournament.

Michelle (sounding deflated)*:* Okay.

DrL: Because that's what we do when we're in love—we give them gifts . . . that doesn't mean you go to the store and buy something. It means you give up something that's very important to you to give them something that's very important to them. O. Henry wrote a short story called "The Gift of the Magi." There was a young couple, very poor, married, and very much in love with each other. Christmas is coming and there is no money to buy gifts for one another. Her prized possession was her long, lovely hair which she had grown since childhood. His prized possession was his solid gold pocket watch—an heirloom, passed down from generation to generation.

Come Christmas morning, she hands her beloved a package. It is a solid gold chain for his pocket watch. He hands his beloved a package. It is a bejeweled comb to hold her beautiful hair in a bun on top of her head. They both cried with joy even though he no longer had the pocket watch, as he had sold it to buy her the jeweled comb, and she no longer had long hair, as she had sold it to buy him the gold chain.

Neither could use the gift the other had given them from a store—but look at the gift each truly got from the other.

Michelle: WOW!

DrL: So when you love somebody you give them what they really need—and your boyfriend needs you to be supportive of the fact that this game is important to his college career—for scholarships. If you do get married, you'll be dancing together for the rest of your lives.

Michelle: That's true. Well, I guess he'll be playing this game and I'll be sitting on the sidelines cheering.

DrL: Good for you! That's the kind of woman a man should marry.

Michelle: Thank you so much, Dr. Laura

Oh, wait a minute, friends! The story does not end there. A few days later I received this e-mail from Michelle:

"A few days ago I called in with a dilemma I had with the prom because my boyfriend's championship lacrosse game

(with college scouts) was the same night. You told me the story of the 'Gift of the Magi,' and that if you really loved someone you would be willing to give up whatever was most important to you—which for me was the prom. I took your advice and called up my boyfriend telling him that we would be going to his lacrosse game instead of senior prom. He explained to me that he knew I would decide to go to his game, so he went ahead and bought our prom tickets so we would go to prom.

"So, basically, I was willing to give up senior prom for him, and he was willing to give up what was most important to him, his championship game—proving the story of 'The Gift of the Magi.'

"But hold on! The story gets better! Yesterday we found out that because of some unknown factor, his championship game was changed from 7 o'clock to 3 o'clock in the afternoon. Is this a God thing? I think so! Now we not only get to go to prom and his lacrosse game, but we have the knowledge that we are both willing to sacrifice what is most important to us because our love is stronger.

"I know that I am only 17, but I think I found a keeper!! Thank you so much for your wonderful advice to let my MAN know how important he is to me. This experience not only made me grow as a person, but is strengthening our relationship as well."

Now, dear friends, even some seventeen-year-olds can understand the beauty and meaning of having somebody care enough about you to put themselves aside for you—that beats every prom and game imaginable. And when you are living this scenario, no matter what grunge is going on in your life, your marriage is PERFECT!

Introduction

This is not your typical marriage manual—not by a long shot. I'm not going to present the usual psychobabble nonsense that has been dominating the marital therapy field since the sixties which condemns masculinity and disdains femininity, considering both some kind of disorder while striving for the destructive lie of unisexuality. This sort of thinking takes the obvious concept of *equality* in the eyes of the law and the Lord, and morphs it into a false concept of *sameness*. In addition to being utterly ridiculous, believing in "sameness" generates a sense of lack of respect for and a denial of your need for the qualities of the other gender. A respect and admiration for the qualities of the opposite gender will feed you in ways you've ignored or never imagined.

Sometimes this book will seem like a smack in the face, other times it will feel like a big hug. But it will always be about the truth: men and women are as different as bananas and peaches. Sure as fruits they have commonality, but differences in texture, consistency, flavor, color, response to heat and cold, and nutritional content dictate a uniqueness that is to be appreciated, not criticized or dismissed in some bizarre notion that it hurts the banana if the peach is pink. I believe that the single most horrible problem for marriages today is the lack of understanding, not only of what is needed by a man in a woman but also what is needed by a woman in a man. The very acceptance of the polarity of masculine and feminine is what makes a tight, loving, long-lasting bond—not the more mundane issues like equal effort in house-keeping.

I remember growing up with the jokes about the "war between the sexes." That war was simply that men wanted sex without marriage and women wouldn't give sex without marriage. Men were clear on the kind of girl they would bring home to mother, and have as mother of their children. That was just a friendly skirmish compared to what the war is today where the feminist demands by women have made, in my opinion, men *and* women have less respect and regard for women, femininity, motherhood, men, masculinity (am I the only one sickened by metro-sexuality?), fatherhood, family commitments, and marriage.

Today's brave new world is frightening. It is a world where abortion is easily available, the creation and wanton destruction of human life reduced to whim. It is a world where instead of marriage, we have shacking up—where two become . . . two. Instead of marital procreation and meaningful intimacy, we have "hooking up," where sex is for recreation; instead of mothers raising their children we have institutionalized day care; and instead of intact families we have women who are unwed mothers by choice or irresponsibility, intentionally denying a father's love and guidance to children, and way too casual multiple divorces and remarriages, with minor children cruising between homes and parental affairs—with no actual homes of their own. Issues of love, commitment, security, self-respect, values, vows, obligations, and responsibilities have become ethereal vapors rather than the promises of a good life.

As a consequence of all these social experiments, and the normalizing of amorality, men no longer visualize "motherhood." Whom do they look to? The nanny? The day care employee? When they think about apple pie, they wonder, "Which grocery?" Men see women as sex objects when women act like unpaid whores and wage earners who will keep working till they drop and buy that BMW. They have become shell-shocked from the anti-male hostility that women have demonstrated since the 1960s. Now it is difficult to find a male who values virginity, purity, and innocence when females dress like babes and perform oral sex and intercourse without even having to be fed dinner; who puts any rational stock in protecting and providing when women have said they can do and be it all without a man? Men now figure they can benefit with less pressure of responsibility and use women to insure the acquisition of more goodies. Who cares about vows—after all, why buy the cow when the milk is free? Who sees any point in sacrificing for what they see are emasculating ball-busters. They think, "Open your own door, get this seat first if you can, get a job so I can relax, you said you're equal so you pay for dinner, you said you could have/do it all . . . so do it!"

Chivalry is largely dead, and feminism is the murderer. It soured both males and females on the joy, awe, wonder, excitement, thrill, satisfaction from, and mystery of femininity and masculinity. The war between the sexes is today an all-out war. Spouses more likely suffer from behavior that resembles sibling rivalry where there is competition for resources and power versus "giving," and "sleeping with the enemy" where men are the "evil empire" and women are self-centered, complaining, and demanding bi★★hes rather than two folks who thank God every day for the blessing of their marital partner and the opportunity to live for something other and outside of themselves.

You may be wondering which came first, the chicken—feminism—or the egg—male selfishness and immaturity. I believe the answer is feminism. From the first day that *The Feminine Mystique* hit the bookstands, feminism did not focus on equal pay for equal work, but on how marriage, husbands, men in general, and children in specific were the enemies and the oppressors of true womanhood. All, and I mean all, women's studies programs in high schools and universities brainwashed women into believing that they diminished themselves with motherhood unless they were just a receptacle for birth and didn't actually raise their own children, and marriage, which was twisted into an acceptance of patriarchal control and domination.

Societal pressures have determined to destroy the truth: a real man needs a real woman to be complete *and* a real woman needs a real man to be complete; which is why you don't get too far into Genesis without a demonstration of the polarity of Adam and Eve and that they are part of each other (i.e., the "rib").

Happily, and hopefully, I have many listeners who are aware of the beauty and wonder of the masculine/feminine polarity and interconnectedness and interdependence that brings the best out of both. Dick, a listener, wrote:

> *"Your regular commentary of the differences between men and women is refreshing in a social atmosphere where dogma insists that there MUST NOT be any difference. A wise man (or perhaps woman, I really don't know) once said that if you want to insult a woman, call her a whore. If you want to insult a man, call him a liar.*
>
> *"Perhaps there would then be some truth to the assumption that a wife who loves her husband is faithful because she loves him, and a husband who loves his wife is faithful because he has promised her that he will be."*

I believe that one of the most egregious problems standing in the way of folks having good marriages today is an almost total lack of understanding, appreciation, and respect for what is feminine and what is masculine—and therefore what it means to be the counterpoint to the other. This is the reason I will spend time reintroducing you to what masculinity and femininity are and how each can bring the best out of the other as well as bring joy and pride in being a man or a woman. Without this understanding, marriage becomes one of two competitive, neutered drones trying to make sense out of the incomprehensible, stumbling in the dark, confused, trying to get love to little avail and ending up with the worst kind of loneliness and bitterness.

The second major issue standing in the way of a satisfying, happy marriage is the level of selfishness that has become acceptable in our society. Debbie, a listener, wrote:

> *"I believe that one of the basic mistakes that men and women make in marriage is a lack of commitment and sacrifice. Nowadays it seems like people are much more committed to their careers, their interests, etc. I think that people see their marriages and children as dispensable and other selfish pursuits as necessary. We live in very selfish times. The true needs of spouses and children are neglected for the wants of one or both spouses. Marriage and children are a huge sacrifice and commitment. The last few generations have not been taught these basic moral principles. Our society has come to believe that momentary pleasure without obligation is the most important of life's pursuits."*

The feeling of love, which I haven't mentioned yet, is a little understood, yet highly valued *emotion*. It is normal for peo-

ple to enjoy that *feeling* of love. Unfortunately, like chemical
addictions, it can become an end in itself, as the self becomes
the center of the universe—like an infant's perception of the
world. "Early love is when you love the way another person
makes you feel. Mature love is when you love the person as he
or she is. . . . It is the difference between passionate and compassionate love." (*Time* magazine 2/15/93, "What is Love")

An anonymous listener wrote to me, *"I think a lot of people
get married to fulfill their own needs, but I think you should get married when you're ready to fulfill the needs of your spouse. I think that
is real love, to want to give to . . . and make someone else happy."*
And making you, dear reader, *happy* in your marriage is my
goal with *The Proper Care and Feeding of Marriage*. And make
no mistake, marriage *is* the best state for men and women. A
new study (Institute for Social Sciences at Cornell University,
12/08/05) shows that people who are married—compared to
those shacking up, or seriously or casually dating—report the
highest levels of well-being, regardless of whether they are happily married or not. "Even when controlling for relationship
happiness, being married is associated with higher self-esteem,
greater life satisfaction, greater happiness, and less distress. The
finding that people in relatively unhappy marriages appeared
to benefit from being married perhaps stemmed from the stability, commitment, and social status of the relationships." I
believe that when many people reported themselves as less than
happily married, they were complaining about some negative,
instead of embracing what is, in the final analysis, the greater
number of good things, but "taken for granted."

Researchers (Brandeis University, 2/14/06) also report
that "men and women in unhappy marriages suffered from
increased stress levels throughout the day at home and at work
as well as higher blood pressure . . . stress has been linked to

a higher risk of heart disease, stroke, cancer, and many other health problems. . . . When there is marital concern, men and women are equally affected."

So here it is: if you're married you're better off mentally and physically; if you're in a happy marriage, you're even more better off!

A listener sent me the obituary of an eighty-nine-year-old man from Arizona who was a minister, a prisoner of war in Germany during World War II, a professor and president of a college, a fisherman and a hunter ("as a way to build strong relationships, teamwork and family ties"). Where the obituary got to the point of his survivors, this is what was written: "MM is survived by his loving wife of 67 years. He was always quick to point out (accurately so) that his accomplishments and decisions were all shared by her. He was fond of saying that they agreed at marriage that he would make all the major decisions and she would make all the minor ones . . . 'and we haven't had a major decision yet.' "

Another listener, M'Liz, sent me a column published in her local newspaper that does a short job bio on folks.

"This gentleman works for a trash company, works long hours, has done it for years, but it is the reason he gives for his motivation that is awesome. It's just like you are always telling us women: our men work hard to take care of their families. It's simple, basic instinct and right. My husband and I just celebrated our 28th anniversary. He is proud to provide enough for us so that I am able to be home with our kids. We all love him for that."

Here is the bio excerpt of a trash collector who works fifty-five to sixty hours a week:

Q: What motivates you to do your best?

A: My family. I work hard because I want to show my appreciation to Irma, my wife of 22 years. I want her to know how much I love her and appreciate all of the times she has prepared my meals and taken care of our kids. I also want to show my children how to become responsible adults regardless of the job they perform.

This, my friends, is a very good man in a quality marriage. Last, a letter from another listener, Julie:

"This was sent to me and I thought you'd get a chuckle out of it—A man called the government office and requested an estimate of his benefits upon retirement. After he got the information, he went on to inquire about his wife's benefits. 'Has she ever worked?' asked the clerk. 'She has worked all her life making me happy,' the man said. 'That's nice,' commented the clerk, 'but has she ever contributed to a pension plan?' 'No,' he said. 'We made an agreement when we got married. I would make the living and she would make the living worthwhile.' "

The man and the woman in this story have a properly cared-for marriage.

People call me every day on my radio program with minor complaints, resentments, confusions, and bitterness in their marriages. With all the different combinations and permutations of people and problems, there are still **three** points I always try to make:

1. Treat your spouse as if you loved them with your last breath—no matter how contrary to that you might feel at any one moment.

2. Think hard every day about how you can make their life worth living.
3. Be the kind of person you would want to love, hug, come home to, and sacrifice for.

Oh, I know what you're thinking: "But MY situation is just so impossible. (S)he makes it impossible. It is impossible to change my feelings or change the situation." Well, my friends, I believe that you will not feel that way by the time you finish *The Proper Care and Feeding of Marriage.* And if you do I can only conclude that one of two possibilities is operating: you might truly need a good divorce attorney, or you are unbearably stubborn! ☺

Chapter 1

"Me Tarzan. You Jane."

The first and most obvious issue in approaching the glory and angst of marriage is to understand the fundamentals of the two people involved; one is a woman, the other is a man. And that is no small thing! Sometimes it must seem to frustrated spouses that each has more genetics in common with flies and daffodils than each other. Not so; but if one doesn't understand, admire, respect, and at times forgive, the nuances of the opposite sex, then the beauty and satisfaction that can arise from the uniting of man and woman in the most important covenant of marriage will not be discovered and enjoyed.

So much sociopolitical time and effort has been spent trying to eliminate the reality, subtlety, magic, and meaning of masculine and feminine, that men and women are afraid and hostile to acknowledge their own pleasure in being such and in yearning for the complementary gender in their spouse.

I remember some twenty-five years ago working with a middle-aged couple on their marital problems. Frankly it seemed as though they were hopeless, refusing to spend any time at all on their difficulties other than complaining and blaming each other for their unhappiness. I recall closing my eyes for a moment and just listening. I could hear the hurt, loss, and need in their voices. Instead of trying to reconcile their "problems" I decided to get to the root of the plant and stop worrying first about the way the petals looked. I opened my eyes and interrupted their fight by saying, slowly, to each of them, "Sir, what do you do to make her feel like a woman?" and "Ma'am, what do you do to make him feel like a man?"

They both just stared at me, speechless. I insisted that they answer my question, despite their determination to get back into the fight. Finally she began to cry softly, and he looked deflated, when just seconds before, they were both energized, reddened with anger. We had some fifteen minutes left to the session, and they had nothing to say—to me or to each other.

Marriages are not business arrangements of coworkers or co-owners. Marriages are the joining of two minds, bodies, souls, spirits, hopes, dreams, needs, personalities, *and* different genders. Unisex clothing does not erase the fact that men and women are very different creatures, and that they are each at their best in enjoying life and love when they revel in those differences with awe and respect.

I did a number of surveys on my Web site (www.drlaura.com). The first had to do with men's and women's perceptions of the opposite sex. For all my questions about men/women, marriage/divorce, and so forth, I received thousands of responses, usually within an hour of my posting the questions! Presented here are, in no order, the most frequently mentioned answers. This first group of answers are from men, and they are about their perceptions and feelings about women *in general*. So you women need to read these with an open heart and mind, for in these answers are many of the solutions to your marital problems with your husbands. The second group of answers are from women, and they are also about women's perceptions and feelings about men *in general*. You men need to read those with the same open heart and mind, if you wish to move your marriage into a more satisfying place in your life.

PART A—ANSWERS BY MEN

Question 1

What do you, as a man, most admire about women in general?

1. Social skills, nurturing nature, compassion, sensitivity, listening skills, focus on relationships and bonding (friends, family, community)
2. Physical softness, sexy, curvy, beautiful, and graceful bodies
3. They will sacrifice for family, the power of creation of new life, being mothers
4. Better at details (multitasking)
5. They take the rough, hard edges off this world, they bring feelings and emotions and a sense of intimacy to us logical guys
6. They can create a home out of any environment, adding aesthetics (color, grace, beauty) to life, they make a house into a sanctuary . . . a home, homemaking
7. The positive effect a good woman can have on her husband and family
8. In femininity there is gentle power over people

Paul, a listener, added: "*What I admire the most among many things in women generally is the strength, inspiration, love, and support they give men. They are the balance that counterweights all the chaos, hard times, and heartache us men go through.*"

I believe that men yearn for their spiritual and psychological counterbalance to humanize and beautify life. I don't think it matters much to a man if his woman chooses to be an accountant or physician—as long as she is "his woman" and "a woman" to him. That understanding is lost to too many women today. Sadly it is all too typical for women to want to be seen by their men *as* the high-powered position they have at work, instead of *as a woman*, with those special attributes that are natural to her and yearned for by her man.

But the reality is that women today do not think of themselves in the context of helping "their man." Women today have been brainwashed into thinking that efforts in that direction are in the category of oppression, subservience, and catering to frail male egos. It is sad that this is the prevalent point of view, because *interdependence* is what ultimately feeds both the man and the woman what they truly need to be happy.

Generally when people lob the phrase "know your place," the understanding is that they are reminding someone of their subordinate position in a relationship or situation. I look at that quite differently. I believe that when a man knows that he actually has a place with his woman, and she with her man, they bring the best out in the other—and enjoy life more feeling purposeful, needed, wanted, and necessary.

What's in it for a woman? Christine, a listener, can tell you: "*My job is just a place I go to for a couple of hours so I can make money. My home is where I live and love and laugh; and so it's very easy for me to make that my number one priority. I get my good feelings from home, not from work.*"

Of course, the work women do can be very important and very satisfying—mine is to me! But, but, but, but the ultimate meaning of my life comes from my position in my family, not my position on any ratings scale or bestseller list.

Question 2
What do you least admire about women in general?

1. Emotional manipulation, complaining, nagging, controlling through "hurt" or "anger," their ability to verbally rip apart your soul, having always to get their way

2. Moodiness, women initially express anger with slamming doors, pouting, and such, and it takes time to find out the root of the matter, bitchy (bossy, superior) attitude
3. Gossip for sense of superiority, catfight with girl friends and female relatives
4. They want to talk everything to death, often without coming to any conclusion or without the intent to actually solve anything
5. Emotions dominate rationality or truth
6. Constant demand for validation, take everything too personally, obsessed with looks (but not for sake of pleasing husbands)
7. Unable to apologize to a man, stay angry and hold grudges a long time, shrillness and fault-finding
8. Inability or unwillingness to understand what a man is, man-hating tendencies these days, not letting the man in their life be a man, too quickly annoyed with the true nature of a man

I'm a woman, and to all these "complaints," I say, "Ouch!" Frankly, ladies, I can attest to these unpleasant traits as valid complaints since I talk mostly to scores of women for three hours each weekday—and I live in the real world. I spend a lot of time trying to remind women of the necessity for them to realize how they are behaving and what a horrendous impact they're making when the "good qualities" they possess as women are exaggerated. For example, in question one, men applaud our "emotional sensitivity." Well, put that in overdrive and we have "emotional chaos" (moodiness, PMS, etc.) overriding our good sense. Men also applaud our social skills, until they get into the arena of our trying to control everything and everybody by having things our way.

It is the smart woman who learns how to temper her emotions and use them wisely. Glenda, a listener, got to that point:

> *"I have to thank you from the bottom of my heart for your book,* The Proper Care and Feeding of Husbands. *I have to say that reading this book was like looking into a mirror. I realized after 16 years of marriage, I have been a horrible wife. I treated my husband like crap and took out my negativity on him, expecting him to always be loving to me while I was a flat-out bitch to him.*
>
> *"I noticed that after many years of verbally beating him down, he became just like me. I have to say, seeing my behaviors in him was not pretty. That was what motivated me to read your book. As I laughed and cried through the chapters, I realized that I had turned a wonderful relationship into a mess. I recognized that my husband was probably one of those men that was just putting up with me for the sake of our children, and that I was on a collision course for divorce when they turned 18.*
>
> *"So, I took your advice . . . I made myself and my home a place that my husband would WANT to come home to. I am pleasant when he walks in the door. I no longer bombard him with whining and bitching. Instead, if I have something that we need to discuss, I ask him to let me know when a good time for us to talk would be. I smile more. Sounds simple, but he made the comment to me that my smile is contagious—it makes his heart melt—so I definitely do more of that. Overall, my relationships with my husband and children have improved beyond belief! For that, I thank you from the bottom of my heart!"*

Notice, please, that all she did was to stop allowing her sensitive, wonderful, womanly capacity for emotionality to overwhelm the loveliness that is in a woman's smile, touch, and attitude. No biggie, in a way. No five years of marital counseling to work out points of contention; just a *positive* use of feminine blessings, instead of letting those blessings run amok for lack of control.

Question 3

What do you most fear in a relationship with a woman?

1. Rejection, abandonment, to fail in her eyes, that I won't be able to keep her happy—that she'll never be satisfied
2. Modern (feminist) women seem to be able to dump their marriages and take their children away from their daddies on a whim: if they feel like it.
3. That she will take me for granted (common, mundane thing) instead of taking care of me, constant put-downs and disrespect, unwarranted criticism to make me over in her image of man/husband, that I will slip away as not being important in her life
4. The loss of physical and emotional closeness and intimacy (warmth and sex), that she will become cold and aloof, infidelity
5. Lack of support and respect, her inability to forgive and forget
6. That I will not be able to take care of her needs in the way she wants done, that I'm not valued in any way other than fulfilling her needs as she has them
7. The changes women go through when going from girlfriend to wife to mother because with each phase they care less and less about their man and more and more about themselves, withholding sex for control

8. Being open and vulnerable and having her use it against me or paraded in front of her friends and mother when she's mad

Clearly men's worries about their wives distill down into one main concept really: loss. Men fear most losing their woman's love, goodwill, loyalty, affection, respect, value—it is all *very* personal and not at all related to housework or physical beauty. I have said this so many times on my radio program and in *The Proper Care and Feeding of Husbands* and *Woman Power,* but it needs frequent repeating: men are very simple creatures; this doesn't mean they are stupid, but it does mean they aren't really very complex. They yearn for the simple things with their woman: affection, approval, and attention. As macho as any man might be, his true sense of "manness" needs reinforcement by his woman. If your man comes home after a horrible defeat at work, and you look into his eyes and tell him, "Honey, I know you will be able to find a way to take care of this situation because I've seen you conquer problems for us so many times over the years. I believe in you," he *will be able* to conquer. If, instead, you yell, scream, put him down, get all depressed, whiny, and blaming, and threaten him with the loss of his family, you'll see quickly that your response was more destructive to his entire being than whatever happened at work. You, yes, you! have that much power with your man. Use it benevolently, with the compassion men admire so much in us.

It is so sad that feminism demoted that singularly magical ability of women to transform deflated men into heroes and warriors into a notion of massaging the frail, pathetic ego of a weak man. In doing so, feminism robbed women of one of their most blessed abilities in life: the ability to not only create life in their wombs, but to sustain that life force in the husbands.

Dawn and Craig called my radio show when she wanted to know how best to support her man.

> **Dawn:** We both feel that it's very important for me to be a stay-at-home mom. However, my husband's job has become just an absolute nightmare for him. He's working full-time and he goes to school full-time. He's trying to get done with school in two months. His job is just a nightmare for him; however, he makes enough money for me to stay home with our baby.

> **DrL:** Well, Craig, that's what a **man** does. I'm proud of you! A **man** doesn't say, "I'm not going to take care of my woman and my kid because I hate my job." A **man** says, "I hate my job, but hell, I'm taking care of my woman and my kid!" You, Craig, are a **real man!**

Craig laughs.

> **DrL:** No, seriously, there aren't a lot of real men around. There are a lot of males, but you're a real man.

> **Craig:** Thanks.

> **DrL:** And the way you support that, Dawn, is to point out to him that he's a real man, and your hero. He is putting up with crap as a man would, to protect and provide for his family. I respect and admire that. I hope you have some sons so he can raise them to be real men too.

Dawn: I agree.

DrL: That's the answer to your question, Dawn. You put your arms around his neck and say, "You're a real man . . . and you're mine!" Craig, does that truly cover it?

Craig (excitedly): That'll do it!

This was a perfect example of what a man can and will do if his woman lets him know that he's her hero, that she knows she can count on him, and that she respects and loves him. Any woman too high on her horse to understand how important her moral support is to her man's masculinity (and willingness to fight the dragons of life), misses out on real woman power— and also misses out on a happy, motivated husband.

Men praised us in question one, saying that we women can multitask like nobody's business. But we have to be careful that this multitasking does not make us deny Copernicus's discovery (that the earth was *not* the center of the universe—and neither are we!). One listener got jolted back out of the black-hole she was sinking into:

"My hubby is a wonderful man. He works hard so I can stay home with our three-year-old daughter. We are now expecting our second child in July. The other night I was whining about being pregnant, having lots to do, and not feeling great. I was complaining about how WE weren't pregnant, I was! My hubby leaned over, took my hand, and looked lovingly into my eyes. Then he said, 'Don't forget—I'm your financial backer!'

"I haven't laughed so hard in ages. It was so sweet. He is

so much more than a paycheck. We are so lucky to have him as a father and husband!"

This could have been a good example of a marriage going bad with the listener getting into "pissing contests" or "sibling rivalry" about who has more work or more importance, denying the lock-and-key nature of a marriage—neither the lock nor the key is functional by itself. A good marriage is about seeing yourselves as a team, not as competitors or enemies.

It is often true that when we women get challenged we can allow ourselves to get swallowed up by those emotions. Stacey's letter clarifies this:

"I recently lost my father to cancer, and that made me focus entirely on my mother and her needs—and not my husband's needs, or my own. I was denying my husband the things that he deserved the most: a happy, loving home. Listening to your show made me realize that I need to put my feelings of sadness aside and not deny my husband his happiness. This past weekend, I made a point to spend the entire time with my husband doing the things he enjoys doing.

"I was sure to give him a kiss on the cheek or a wink whenever he looked my way. This in turn opened the flood gates of seduction. After spending a wonderful evening with my husband, we made love for the first time in months. Afterward, my husband looked at me and said, 'I missed you.'

"I had finally realized that all this time this wonderful man was understanding and supportive, and here I was not paying attention to his needs. Sure the house was clean and the food was on the table, but he didn't receive the 'love' he so greatly deserved.

"So, thank you so much for opening my eyes to seeing how much a little bit of affection can make US BOTH feel better. I started out just wanting him to feel better . . . little did I realize how wonderful it would make me feel in return."

What scares me to death is what would have happened to this couple had they gone to your typical marital therapy. He would have been cut to ribbons for even having any needs for her, when she is going through mourning. She would have been reinforced in taking care of herself and her mother and leaving him on his own to be "understanding." Their marriage might have been destroyed, or minimally, seriously damaged.

Instead she reinforced her marriage as her first priority, she respected that her husband's needs were not irrelevant simply because she had pain, and she took care of her man, discovering that this fed back to her tenfold. You get by giving—and not by hoarding.

Too often, women look at their husband's needs as a curse and burden, instead of a blessing and oasis from which to derive sustenance.

Question 4
What is the single, most important expectation you have in a wife?

1. A woman who will put family first; create a home/sanctuary for the family; organize household to be a loving mother and raise our children
2. To be understanding and committed—and not easily swayed by external influences on the marriage; loyalty
3. Friend and lover first . . . mother second
4. Trust and faith in me (decisions, actions, etc.); respect

who I am (not try to change me into something she'd
like better)

5. That she makes me her knight in shining armor; admire
me as a husband and a *man*; appreciates what I do for the
family

6. To be trustworthy and loyal; not to see divorce as the
simple solution to problems; be committed to working
through problems not just complaining about them

7. To be my support/cheerleader; stand by me in tough
times; make me feel loved, wanted, and needed; encourage me to be/do my best

8. Make sexual intimacy/love a priority; loving and affectionate even and especially when there is stress

The very day I was compiling this list from the survey responses,
I received a call from a dear woman who holds a powerful corpo-
rate position in a major company. She told me that her twenty-
year relationship was probably coming to an end. She said, "I
think some men just have a tough time being comfortable with
a powerful woman." I gently replied, "I don't think the problem
they have is with her being powerful. I think the problem they
have is when that *powerful woman* doesn't know how to be just *his
woman* when she comes home." After a moment or so, she softly
replied, "Yes . . . that's probably true."

This list from men, about what they most expect from a wife,
is not about their *demands*—it shows clearly how much men
need their women. Real men don't have superiority complexes:
"I am the man, therefore I am more important and you should
bow to me," is not at all what this list demonstrates. This is a list
showing incredible vulnerability because it shows how *dependent*
men are on their women for self-esteem, motivation, purpose
and acceptance, approval and love.

Real men truly value their women and put them back on the pedestal that feminism knocked down. Reuters (5/3/06) published an article about a "study" that concluded that the yearly value of an at-home mom's work is $134,121. The point of putting a dollar amount on all her duties is presumably to give "value" to homemakers' responsibilities where there is none. I believe it is the feminists, and not the husbands, who don't value homemakers.

The same day this study was published, I received many e-mails like the following:

> *"This morning I heard on the radio that the worth of a woman's work for the family was $134,000. Thinking this was great, I thought I'd call my husband from the car. He was home. Well, I did, and his comment was, 'Oh, yeah,' and not enthused. So I quickly left the subject and continued on home. Well, when I rounded the corner, he was just leaving. I thought, 'Why couldn't he have waited another 30 seconds to see me! Hummmphhh!'*
>
> *"When I walked in, I saw a note for me. This is what it said. 'Cheryl, the study was wrong about how much housewives are worth. They sought to put a price tag on how much your work is worth, but I say you are priceless. There is no amount of money in the world that could replace you. No amount of money could give me the peace of mind you give me knowing that you are taking care of the kids, not just their physical needs—but also being there for their emotional and spiritual needs, and they know they can count on you always.*
>
> *"'You also are always there for me, to love me and to take care of me and to hold me. I want you to know that I love you for all you do and even more, for your desires, because you want to do these things instead of spending your time elsewhere. I am*

blessed by God because you are in my life! I hope you have a great day! I love you, Eric.'

"*I will have a great day, Dr. Laura. Thank you for letting me share my blessings.*"

So the study purports that replacing a homemaker with a professional for each task she does would come up to $134,000? Really? And what about the love . . . what price is love? And what professional could come into the home and create that warmth, love, and glorious family feeling? Financial compensation is not the best compensation for the heart and soul.

I suppose that this listener's husband, Eric, could hire a slew of folks to take on her tasks, but he wouldn't look at them with the awe, respect, admiration, love, appreciation, and passion with which he looks at her.

All husbands, though, should write "Eric letters" to their wives and not do the Archie Bunker routine of thinking that she should know how you feel about her value to you simply because you're still there or not complaining. A letter like Eric's is as elevating to her as her support and love is elevating to you.

Question 5

What is the most important thing you think modern women don't get about being a woman?

1. That chivalry and gentlemanly behavior is a good thing; to enjoy being a woman and let men treat them as such; that men are not the enemy
2. There is value in being wife and mother; they have given up the need to be needed, loved, and cherished
3. They treat men as inferior, yet they spend their lives try-

ing to act like men; women's lib ought not to be about free sex, aborting surprises, and being tough and angry

4. That "it" is not all about her feelings and desires; they are more consumed with "what's in it for me" than concerned about taking care of their man; that it is better to be loved than to be right all the time

5. That there are differences between men and women—and that those differences are complementary—and that's why they need each other; equality does not imply sameness; modern women don't seem to accept their own human, feminine nature and they fight their natural inclinations; femininity is not a disease to be cured; value, morals, and modesty are important

6. Physical attractiveness is only a spark—being cheerful and loving is the flame; being kind, courteous, and respectful; the importance of sex in a relationship

7. They have all the power in a relationship to make or break it; how strongly they can influence a man, make him feel like a man; men are simple creatures and need only sex, food, and appreciation; that being loving to your husband does not make you a slave; you catch more flies with honey than nags

8. They think men and women don't really need each other; they think they can do it all (job, kids, house, and last and least, husband); that being a mother and wife is more important than any job or career

How could it be so that several generations of women don't appreciate the value and power of their femininity? How is it that women would yearn to throw away their magnificent importance as the center of family, community, and life itself? The answer? Feminism! Feminism has been a scourge upon the land and upon women, children, men, and ultimately, families and society.

The true ideal of feminism—that men and women should have the same rights and opportunities—is an obvious positive civil rights issue. But that is not the feminism that has ever dominated. The feminist movement as such was totally co-opted by a mentality that despised femininity, motherhood, wifehood, and men in all forms except castrated.

Michael, a listener, submitted this letter in response to my on-air query, "In what way(s) would you consider yourself a recovered feminist and what parts of the feminist agenda have you dropped and why?"

"I am married to a feminist psychology professor—envy me. My life under the feminist Taliban has been a mixture of guilt mingled with hopelessness and despair. I have been less than a plow horse. To be a man was to be blamed for everything, appreciated for nothing. Rescuing her and her sibling's lives, buying her a 4,000 sq. ft., six-bedroom house on a hill with a view earned me a 'performs as expected' as a husband.

"I started listening to your show to better understand my wife and her career—and instead, ended up understanding myself. I like me now. I have value. My needs and feelings are not scummy. I am no longer devastated by her displeasure. Although I no longer believe that women can actually have feelings of love and admiration for us men, (with your show) I have hope for my sons. I love your book The Proper Care and Feeding of Husbands *and appreciate you more than you could ever know. Of course, my wife and daughter hate you, hate your book, and hate me for buying it and 'shoving it in their faces' (their words).*

"Thank you for the happiness and the possibility of joy."

Sadly I received hundreds of such letters from sad, lost, unloved, and unappreciated men, who nonetheless worked very hard to try to make their women happy, obviously against great odds.

How and why did the feminist movement create such enmity for men? First it is important to recognize that the enmity was also directed at women—a kind of self-loathing of nurturing breasts, life-producing uterus, and an emotionally sensitive, nurturing spirit.

This is something Erica, another listener, can tell you about:

> *"As an 18-year-old high school student, I participated in my first women's studies class. It made me feel ANGRY and POWERFUL. I suddenly became a militant feminist. In college, I continued with these classes, and fit right into the liberal, left-wing, feminist culture—participating in many feminist marches and rallies, including anti-anti-abortion demonstrations.*
>
> *"Then I met my husband, a Christian and anti-abortion. I found him irresistible—partly because I wanted to convert him to my side. Funny thing is, he changed me to his. Before I knew it, I was in love with him. I wanted to be and do everything for him, if only because he was the MAN I loved. I was happy to cook for him. I'd bring his laundry over and wash/fold while we watched movies on Sunday afternoon. I gave him back rubs after a stressful day. And, do you know what?! He repaid all my kindnesses and more. He'd run out and buy me ice cream in the middle of the night when I was studying for finals; he'd come by my house and drive me to school on rainy mornings; he'd take me to see a 'chick flick' and to a sushi dinner and love every moment of it because he was with me.*

"Now that we're married, we continue putting all our efforts toward taking care of each other's needs. I've never felt myself so fulfilled and happy. I know that as an ANGRY feminist (any other kind?) I would never have experienced the joy of giving fully and having the faith that I will always be safe, loved, and taken care of.

"I still believe that men and women have equal VALUE, but VERY different ROLES. I'm GRATEFUL that I can take such good care of my husband. I am GRATEFUL to be feminine and womanly. I am GRATEFUL that my husband and I don't vie for power in the relationship, but humbly give to each other. I am PROUD that I am my husband's wife, and look forward eagerly to also being my kids' mom.

"I've given up my ANGER towards MEN. I've stopped wanting to FEMINIZE males. I even LIKE it now if a gentleman opens the door for me. I always smile graciously and say, 'Thank you.' I wish there were more gentlemen in this world—I'm so glad I married one. I've given up my hateful 'feminist ideals' and now I live in bliss with a REAL MAN, as a REAL WOMAN."

Of the thousands of responses I received—within twelve hours!—to my question about being a Recovered Feminist, there were a handful of familiar themes:

- *"Everything I want, what makes me happy as a woman (being at home, family, having children, having a knight in shining armor) is spit upon by two groups: chauvinists and feminists. They're one and the same, aren't they? Vile, loathsome, selfish people . . . ironic that they don't like each other either."*

- *"I realize that it is not submissive to let my husband be a man and not expect him to act like my girlfriend. I realize that being feminine is much more powerful than being a feminist."*

- *"I finally realized how self-centered I had become as a feminist. My complete focus was on MY happiness, MY problems, MY agenda, and MY future. I thought his job was to do everything to please ME. Since reading* The Proper Care and Feeding of Husbands, *I have been focusing on HIM more. It is such a delight to me to see how much happier he has become. I continue to enjoy my release from my 'feminist prison.' "*

- *"Feminists can't see power in being a true woman who uses her God-given natural abilities to nurture both children and a husband. I know how marriages can suffer if both spouses are working, exhausted, and too tired to tend to the relationship. I've come full circle on pretty much every feminist issue there is—and I'm no longer arguing with my nature on these issues. I'm no longer fighting to prove that I am not a 'typical woman' and, as a matter of fact, I quite like it."*

- *"Feminists abandoned all the virtues of womanhood (modesty, tact, subtlety, civility) and adopted all the vices of men (promiscuity, vulgarity, aggressiveness). Perhaps this would be less appalling if the feminists adopted at least some of the male virtues (logical thought, adherence to principles, stoicism, reticence), but they have not. Paradoxically, feminism today is about hating men, but at the same time encouraging detestable behavior in men: how, exactly, has abortion on demand improved male/female relationships?"*

- *"How am I a recovered feminist? Let me count the ways:*
     "I no longer: look down on motherhood, open doors when my husband is with me, expect my husband to tolerate my

irrational emotions, think men are pigs, look up to female CEOs who leave their babies to others to raise and love, and I no longer apologize for my conservative and traditional values. In other words, I am much happier being a woman rather than wishing I was a man. God does not make mistakes."

- *"I was raised to believe that I could be all and do all. That philosophy soon crashed into reality. I had a career, a husband, a child, and a home—and I expected to be able to manage it all. With great fatigue, I realized I was doing a pretty poor job of it. Then I realized the feminist movement had robbed us all. Before the feminist brainwash, women stayed home to love their children. Husbands were proud to care for and provide for their families. The woman had time and energy to devote to the pride and care of home and family. Wanting to return to such a life, I ran into the feminist agenda: my husband expected me to have all and do all. He, brought up in feminism, was not prepared to shoulder the responsibility of being the sole financial support for the family. After some problems in day care, that issue was resolved. I am now a stay-at-home mom, and together, my husband and I are raising our children. The feminist lie has been ousted—and we are living the truth."*

Both men and women are confused about the proper source of their self-worth, how to relate to one another, how to find happiness when feeling pulled in too many directions, and how to find peace and security in love with the opposite sex when they don't know how to be or what to expect or what is expected. It is very positive to elevate and celebrate the qualities of men or women—but NOT at the cost of the health of the other, children, relationships, and society.

I have said for quite a while that feminism robbed women of their essence and their ability to find pure joy and happiness. Yes it is a good thing that a woman can run a company; it is a bad thing if she does this while neglecting her husband and children. She will ultimately suffer when she realizes that her life choices have made her a worker drone, and not a full, feminine human being.

As Marla relates:

"I used to be a card-carrying feminist. I've now come to realize that all the power IS ours if we just embrace being a REAL woman. I love my man. I stand behind my man. By making him more important than me and considering his feelings above mine, it actually works out that I get everything I could possibly want. I adore doing things for him because I love him. I don't have anything to prove about so-called equality anymore. I love being my man's woman. I love him opening doors and his heart to me. Being a real, true woman has brought me more happiness than any amount of feminism or liberation ever could. I am a very loved woman and that is because I truly love my man."

Jae, a listener, summarized this all quite beautifully:

"A real woman is someone who has no shame in being a wife and a mother, and puts her career on hold until the kids are grown. A real woman is available emotionally, spiritually, and physically for her man. She is selfless, and in doing so, loves herself because she has so much to offer."

Did you read that? "She is selfless, and in doing so, LOVES HERSELF BECAUSE SHE HAS SO MUCH TO OFFER." Wow!

The simplicity of Jae's letter is stunning. And it speaks to the truth.

As I've mentioned, women are no longer programmed to admire and respect what is masculine and manly. Nonetheless, when asked, it is stunning how "retro" the answers are. That is because what is hard-wired into feminine and masculine DNA and hearts is a need, a yearning for the completion of their beings: the interdependence of masculine and feminine. Part B, women's answers, reveals that truth.

PART B—ANSWERS BY WOMEN

Question 1

What do you, as a woman, most admire about men in general?

1. Hardiness, physical strength, masculinity, mental toughness, protective, courage, self-confident, persevering, emotional strength when facing fear
2. Ability to see the whole picture objectively, think logically, get things done, practicality
3. Honest, straight to the point, backbone, strength of character and opinion, uncomplicated
4. They get over things fast, can be friends with other men who have hurt their feelings (not petty, catty, or gossipy), bond easily, don't make everything a crisis, up front with anger, don't overanalyze everything
5. Provider for family, responsible, driven to fix and help, leadership and devotion
6. Chivalry, gentlemanly behavior, willingness to slay dragons every day, they will sacrifice everything to make their woman happy
7. They are put together nicely and their passion in sex, they are comfortable with their bodies
8. Their simplicity

As I look at this list, I see that the answers were focused on the pragmatic. This is not an accident. I believe that women crave the bedrock characteristics that are "masculine." That is true in spite of cultural pressures working against women appreciating masculinity and having appreciation and respect for what a "man" can offer. In counterpoint to Maureen Dowd's book *Are Men Necessary?* Lori Borgman wrote in a syndicated column, "There are a lot of things I sometimes think I'd like to be, but a man is never one of them. Talk about a group maligned, vilified and marginalized. For the most part—abusers, perverts and slackers aside—most men are stand-up guys. They work hard. They create, tinker, build, engineer and achieve. They take carping, criticizing and complaining on the chin, and rarely get the thanks they deserve."

Liz, a self-proclaimed "recovering feminist" and listener, wrote:

"Everywhere one turns today, men are demeaned. After listening to your radio program and reading The Proper Care and Feeding of Husbands, *I've been appalled at what I now 'notice' in our media: Heating commercial—husband portrayed as the bumbling idiot, who needs the wife's wisdom to choose the right unit; GPS unit commercial—husband portrayed as the idiot who won't ask for directions. Woman saves the day with GPS; insurance commercial—wife talks wisdom with a friend while husband blows up barbecue. . . . I could go on ad-nauseam. Recognizing that many of the above references are 'just to be funny,' I see this as an alarming trend. Feminists would scream if this behavior were directed toward women. It's open season on men in our culture."*

The main problem with these cultural influences is that they result in a constant IV drip of negativity into the veins of women who then treat their men with reflexive, almost unconscious disdain—and then call me nonplussed that their husbands ignore Valentine's Day and anniversaries. I tell them, "Happily married men always remember sentimental holidays." Silence. I add, "So tell me why your husband is unhappily married?" Usual response is, "I don't know." If I nag some more, I can get to the answer, "Well, I guess, maybe . . ." The list I get to includes: no validation, no affection, no sex, lots of complaining, chaotic schedules and lack of warm home atmosphere, arguments about minutia mostly started by dissatisfied, unhappy wife, payback punitive, hurtful behaviors, and so forth. When did we forget that you catch more flies with honey?

With this list, I am happy to announce that at least my female listeners have some appreciation for what is manly, male, and masculine. However when women do acknowledge wanting a man "they can count on," they get grief from the feminists.

For example, the *Los Angeles Times* in February 2006 published an article titled "It Turns Out Money Can Buy Love, After All." The "spin" of this article is obviously obnoxious: "men want a woman with a good sense of humor, while women prefer a guy who has a steady job and pays his bills on time. 'And they say money can't buy you love,' quipped a [female] financial planner."

The truer point is that women are not gold diggers; women want a man who can provide financial security so that she will be able to take care of their children at home! All throughout the animal kingdom, the males have to prove something to the females in order to get one to mate with him; some species have to build acceptable nests, others have to fight competitors; human men need to be able and willing to be sole support.

Every call I have ever gotten from a woman who was the breadwinner was filled with her pain, jealousy, and resentment that she wasn't the one at home with the children. I believe that no matter how financially successful and powerful a woman is, she naturally wants to be protected and provided for by her man—it is what makes her feel more womanly.

Women want a man they can lean on. However feminism has brainwashed women to believe that all men are inconsiderate beasts you can't rely on. Therefore, the threat goes, never give up your independence. This mentality has confused and frightened women into an avoidance of becoming dependent on their men. So to protect themselves, women ferociously parry with their men, while denigrating their own desires to tend the home and raise children. Then they call me all depressed and angry . . . and they think it is because of their husbands.

I recently took a call from a woman who waited until thirty to marry. She quit her job and is at home with their one-year-old son. She called me with exactly this dilemma. Her father had been a loser—at least that is what her mother always told her. And now she's wondering if she did a good thing by marrying a man she sees as so controlling. When I asked her to describe him, what came back was the very definition of a responsible man.

I believe that what has happened is that the healthy part of her picked a man she could count on. The unhealthy part of her won't believe it, is scared of the vulnerability of losing her independence, and comes up with a good reason to avoid turning herself over to him—that's the part of her that is hurt and confused by her childhood experiences. It would seem that there are only two choices: one, guy is loser she can't count on, and two, guy is controller who will consume her. There is a place in between.

She was an extremely intelligent woman and understood the concepts but wasn't quite sure how to put it on the emotional level so that she could think and feel better things. I suggested that the moment he came home from work, she greet him at the door and then ask him to stand still. She was to turn her back to him, tighten up her body, put out her arms like an airplane, and just let herself fall backward toward him. I told her that he would do what a real man does for his woman and family, he would catch her.

The next morning I got this e-mail from Sophie, another listener:

> "I listened to the caller who was having trouble trusting her man. Your solution was to have her play the 'trust game,' where she would fall into her husband's arms and trust that he would catch her. I played that game last night with my husband. I simply said, 'Do what comes naturally,' as you instructed the woman to do. I turned around, stepped a foot away, fell back . . . and he caught me. He then proceeded to kiss me. He shrugged and said, with smile, 'I did what came naturally. You were in my arms and I had to love you.'
>
> "Dr. Laura, I thought you might like to know—it was a good night!"

Question 2
What do you least admire about men in general?

1. Hard for them to give-and-take in discussion, they want to give the answer, not figure it out together

2. That they can have casual sex; obsession with women's bodies/sex; shallow physical attraction to women
3. Pride (male ego); not good with criticism; won't admit weaknesses; arrogance; emotional neediness
4. Too easily pussy-whipped by intimidating women and/or their mothers
5. Don't wish to do domestic work; expect women do to child-rearing
6. Workaholics; can't multitask; focus on bigger picture, and not on details
7. Crude humor and admiration of violence; sloppy
8. Won't talk about feelings—won't show many feelings besides anger; not sensitive to feelings of woman; won't easily vocalize love and appreciation

It's interesting. These criticisms are largely another way of looking at the compliments. For example, in question one, answers included men are stoic, take charge, protect, don't personalize everything. In question two, all that got turned into not expressing emotions, want to fix things without talking about it, aren't sensitive enough. This must feel to men like a "make up your mind" moment!

One of the criticisms aimed at me since *The Proper Care and Feeding of Husbands* hit the bookstores in 2003 is that I seem to think men are perfect and that women are always at fault for marital problems. I do understand that perspective coming from defensive wives and rabid feminists (sorry for redundancy). For the others who are perplexed at my apparent proman bias, you are seeing the truth! As a woman, I am honest and embarrassed to say that over the last half century, the tide has turned seriously hostile and demeaning toward men and masculinity. As a result, women, in my opinion, behave proportionally more destructively and insensitively in relationships and marriages than have men, and men are less and less behaving like *men*.

However, be very clear that I don't see men as perfect—if that were so, I wouldn't be having daily on-air arguments with some damsel about her ridiculous choice of a scummy, alcoholic, druggie, irresponsible, philandering, violent, self-centered, momma's boy of a boyfriend. But, and it is a big but here so take notice, I think when a damsel picks your basic nice guy, she is generally handicapped in realizing the power she has to turn him from a toad to a prince at a moment's notice with a kiss and a loving compliment. Most women today, I fear, see and treat their men like an accessory in their marriage instead of God's contribution to their happiness.

Yeah, guys in bunches are crude—but your basic decent guy turns it off in front of a lady . . . get it? LADY. Guys have testosterone and a brain wired for appropriate aggression—but your basic guy uses that aggression in sports, business, and war. Issues of guys being interested in the visual with respect to women, or having sex are important—that is built into the wiring of a male, as breast-feeding and bonding are built into the wiring of a female. Would women like to hear as a criticism that they spend much too much time on the interpersonal versus the intellectual?

Men and women are complementary—perfection is created by their union. It does no good to ridicule what is inherent in the male and female; save that for the neurotic.

Men need women to help them be civilized, focused, ambitious, connected, healthy, and happy. Women are men's anchors and connection to the sublime of love, family, and meaning in life.

When women learn to look at a man's nature as something they contribute to instead of eliminating, women will have happier selves, men, and marriages.

Instead most women want their men to be just like them. Look at the list again: it contains descriptions of what a woman is! This is why I believe this book is so important; women and men must learn to have a sense of humor about, and a respect for, what is not themselves.

Lisa, a divorced listener, who hopes to meet a good man after her youngest graduates, wrote:

> *"I lost my father early in the year and admired him greatly, as well as other men of his age. He was 83, grew up in poverty, had a broken home with a mother who married several men, all of whom were less than gracious to my father.*
>
> *"Yet, he grew up to be the kind of man that stood up for his convictions, he told you like it was, pretty matter of fact. He worked hard and was proud. He raised me to be a competent woman, yet he expected me to be treated like a lady.*
>
> *"I do not care that Dad wasn't in touch with 'his feminine side.' These men demonstrated for the most part accountability for their actions. The best men I know today all have said their fathers were more than a little hard on them—it's because they were raising them to be the men they are today."*

Your basic decent guy, ladies, is a guy! So don't expect him to talk in paragraphs when men deal with pointed sentences; don't expect him to sniffle over a chick flick or your girl friend's problems or the sixth rendition of your hurt feelings—men handle things and get on with it; don't expect him to not want your body in rapturous passion—men show and receive love through that very tight connection . . . without flowers.

Question 3

What do you most fear in a relationship with a man?

1. Rejection; infidelity; he will get tired of me sexually; I will disappoint him (poor housekeeping, bad mother, not good with money, too independent, get old and wrinkled, etc.)
2. I won't understand him; coming across as a nag; take him for granted so he falls out of love with me
3. Being controlled; lose getting my own way; lose myself to make him happy
4. Physical and/or mental abuse
5. Not being "happily ever after"
6. "I'm nervous about meeting my husband's sexual needs. I know this is how he likes love to be expressed, and it has taken me a long time to realize that this is just as important to him as loving and talking and hugging is to me."
7. Involvement with pornography

The overwhelming response was number one. Over 95 percent of the women who answered this question were most in fear of being rejected and abandoned. This is an issue I deal with a lot on my program—and not because it is a typical male behavior. Of course it is sometimes true that some women select a husband poorly, picking an immature guy because they think they can fix him, or a narcissistic guy because they are charmed by him; this results in a man they cannot count on.

For the most part the insecurity that is expressed by my female callers has to do more with their underlying recognition that they are not behaving in a way that bonds their men to them. It usually takes severe badgering on my part to get them to look at and accept this truth. One recent female caller was telling me about her problems with "rage attacks." It turns out that he installs kitchens, and she is concerned that some babelike single woman client of his will seduce him away from her. I asked her if she thought screaming at a man would make him feel more loved, connected, and happy in his marriage. "No," she said, "but I don't know what else to do. I get scared." Another woman called to complain that her husband ignored their thirtieth anniversary. I told her, "No happily married man forgets his anniversary; for him it is a monument to his joy!" Not surprisingly she couldn't/wouldn't deal with his unhappiness—just about how hurt and disappointed she was.

The very next morning I received this e-mail from John, a listener, who has the answer for both these wives:

> *"The other day my wife and I had the good fortune to catch part of your show while driving home from work early. We heard the caller who was complaining about how her husband had completely ignored her 30th wedding anniversary. I find that hard to believe, and thought you may appreciate a man's point-of-view.*
>
> *"How could her husband possibly ignore the fresh cut flowers in the living room when he got home from work? How could he ignore the perfume she was wearing, or the outfit she had on? Or that she had cooked his favorite meal, or in the least made reservations at their favorite restaurant. How could her husband possibly ignore the candles, or the bath that she had drawn for them to share, or the lovemaking that followed such a wonderful evening? Or even the hotel reservations that she had booked for them.*
>
> *"Oh . . . I know . . . none of those things happened. She*

simply sat there and expected their anniversary to be another birthday party for her. She forgot that an anniversary is about celebrating their lives together, not an opportunity to get another piece of jewelry she had her eyes on. It isn't about things. It's about each other.

"I guess her husband didn't have much to celebrate."

It is typical of most marital therapy to spend months going over every harsh word said and every stupid deed done—this immerses folks in the negative. Instead go right ahead and create the positive. If you wish to stay together, commit to being your best dream, not your worst nightmare. It's the people who relish hanging on to the hurts and the power that gives them over their spouse, that never salvage nor create beauty in their marriages.

Question 4
What is the single most important expectation you have for a husband?

1. Listening and remembering what I say
2. To make me feel loved and cherished
3. To be a loving husband and father; that he is primarily committed to family; faithful and loyal; a kind heart; be spiritual
4. To be my superfan; be my best friend
5. Financial security
6. To be appreciative and not just expect
7. Leader in the household and make family-wise decisions; comfortable with being head of the family without being cruel, bossy, controlling, or overbearing; a positive role model; to slay dragons

8. Faithful—no affairs (emotional or physical) and no pornography

Unless it was included under answer 2, not one woman
mentioned sexual intimacy. I recently received this e-mail from
Michelle:

"It seems like your book The Proper Care and Feeding
of Husbands *should have been titled* Have Sex With Your
Husband . . . *so he won't leave you; so he'll pay attention to
the kids; so he'll fix the bathtub; so he'll buy you something
nice. I've heard it all on your show. It makes me very sad. It
sounds like marriage is a lot like prostitution, using sex to get
something to have power. No woman should have to get it on
all the time so her husband will participate in the family. There
is so much more to life than getting naked and doin' it."*

I e-mailed her back: "Prostitution is receiving money for
anonymous sex. Marital sex is about love and bonding."

Some women *expect* to be cherished, protected, and provided for by a man without that man enjoying the depth of
passion that makes him feel loved, needed, wanted, adored,
and ultimately accepted; that doesn't work for long. A man
needs the physical to feel connected emotionally to his woman,
and by extension, the family. Any woman who dismisses that
truth about her man will lose her man—even if he doesn't
walk out the door until the children are in college.

Question 5
*What is the most important thing you think modern men don't get
about being a man?*

1. Vulnerability is okay (at least with your woman)
2. The need to be a good provider; not expect wife to be just another paycheck
3. To be old-fashioned gentlemen; chivalry is still in demand
4. We still need you to be our heroes
5. Being kind, gentle, and considerate doesn't mean they are "whipped"
6. No "metro-sexuality"—good old masculinity!
7. Responsibility to wives and children versus own personal needs
8. Mothers should be home with their children

This list just goes to prove a point I keep on making: the "times" are irrelevant to the true needs of men and women to be true to their own natures. Please stop making politically correct social agendas out of the simple needs of a woman for a man and a man for a woman. Please stop trying to understand the opposite sex as though they were a bug to dissect. It is important to accept and respect what is masculine and feminine without envy or negativity. And, it is essential to support what is the ultimate truth in each other: you both are a blessing to each other—SHOW IT!

Toni, a listener, wrote this e-mail to me:

"I just want to thank you, Dr. Laura, for your program and for what you do—but more specifically, for what your program does for my marriage. This may sound strange, but I have actually never heard your program, but my husband has. His job requires him to travel frequently, so he listens to the radio quite a bit. Many times he has come home and held me tight and

*spoke genuine words of appreciation for me as his wife and the
mother of his children.*

*"He then proceeded to explain to me how he has been lis-
tening to Dr. Laura and realized how blessed he truly is. So, I
don't know what you're doing or exactly how you're impacting
my husband, but please, keep it up!!"*

And another e-mail from Nicole, who took my on-air advice
and can't believe how much happier she is in her marriage. Her
husband is a gun enthusiast, and like most women, she wasn't at
all interested in going to a shooting range for entertainment. After
listening to my program she decided one day to offer to him a day
at the range with her! Turns out they had an excellent time and
his enthusiasm for teaching her made her smile.

The very next day she received this e-mail from him:

*"Hey, I just wanted to tell you thanks for being such a great
wife and companion. I don't know any guy who has such a
beautiful, funny, caring, intelligent, sexy, loving wife as I do
and one who will not only get involved in the things I like, but
be truly interested. I am truly the luckiest man alive. I'm sorry
I don't always reciprocate, and I'll work harder to do better.
You mean everything to me and I will try harder to be worthy
of you. Thanks for everything you do and everything you are.
Love, your husband."*

And all because she went to the shooting range with him.
Nicole feels *"like the luckiest woman alive!"*

Your assignment, dear friends, is to reread this chapter, paying primary attention to the lists made out by the opposite
sex. Without arguments, lengthy discussions, endless hours of
therapy airing complaints, pains, disappointments, threats, and

demands—JUST DO what you know your spouse needs and wants to feel important to you—what you know any woman or man would appreciate. It will, as these last two letters have shown, be lovingly reciprocated.

Or you can dig in your heels, pout, and plan "payback," and, I'm sorry, to what end? Oh yes, "end" may sadly be the correct term.

Chapter 2

"I've Met the Enemy . . . and It's ME!"

Through all the years I was in private practice as a marriage, family, and child therapist, I never once had folks walk in and point to *themselves* as a/the problem with the marriage; not once. When couples or individuals call in to my radio program to address their marital issues, one of the very first things I do is to ask, "What do *you* do to hurt your spouse personally and/or the marriage in general?" It is amazing how capable people are to place blame anywhere else but with themselves. This is not to say that the other person is not contributory; this is to say that it is easier to get your spouse to take responsibility if you role model doing such! Also the only control each one of us has in our relationships is over ourselves.

What I tell callers is, "Look at it this way—if you are causing some problems in your marriage, it is good news and bad news. The bad news is obvious: you're being a pain. The good news is not so obvious: you have the power to change, and in doing so, bring happiness and pleasure to yourself and your family faster than if it is your spouse who is the problem since we can't force anyone to change!"

Why do people so quickly see the other as the enemy when
once they saw the other as *the* antidote to all life's negativities
and the ultimate source of happiness? The answer lies in the
question. When people come together, there is a romantic,
albeit somewhat naïve, immature, or desperate notion that this
joining will fill holes in their souls and psyche. Actually that is
ultimately true, but *only* when each is aware of and understands
the meaning of their own emotional "issues" and is similarly
aware and sensitive to the same in their spouse.

My three decades of experience dealing with people struggling with intimacy tells me that too much of marital therapy
is dealing with marital structure, disappointments, and dis-
enchantments with one's spouse, and not enough on understanding the dueling inner dynamics of spouses. By "inner
dynamics" I mean the complex web of the impact of their
earlier family experiences tangled up with their repetitive,
and largely unproductive, ways of handling real and/or imagined fear and hurt.

In this regard, it is most interesting that many people wonder about their ability to change! Do they truly think personal
change is impossible? Of course not. I believe that what they
are really worried about is whether they will be *safe* and *loved*
if they change. Most people behave "badly" because they are
struggling with those core concerns. They are concerned that
if they change they might not be loved and won't be safe from
hurt . . . like they were in their pasts.

Phillip, a caller to my program, was confused about just
these issues.

> ***Phillip:*** I don't know where to start. I'm trying to save my
> marriage. I'm trying to find out whether or not it's pos-
> sible for me to change. I want to change so badly.

DrL: What is it you'd like to change?

Phillip: My outlook and my attitude and how I treat my wife and my child. I am so demeaning to them and I don't give them the respect they deserve. I see what I'm doing but I still do it.

DrL: Explain to me how at the very moment you know you're being a snotty, nasty bastard, that you don't go, "Oh my God, I'm sorry!" I just want to know what's going on in your head at that very moment when you see and hear yourself and you don't stop.

Phillip: Wow! That's a good question. Maybe I realize that I've lost control of the situation.

DrL: Okay, so what I learned from you is that when you're at a point in which you're making a choice between feeling in control or being a good man—you're choosing being in control. That means being in control is the most overwhelming concern. That's an anxiety reaction. Where do you think that comes from?

Phillip: My parents were separated twice during my childhood and then finally when I was twelve it was over between them. My mother was an alcoholic. I could ramble on forever . . . my life was out of control during my childhood.

DrL: What do your daughter and wife do that makes you feel out of control as a parent and husband?

Phillip: Lazy and messy.

DrL: So you need order in your life because you're still trying to survive your childhood even though you're not in your childhood any longer?

At this time I took a commercial break and suggested to Phillip that he think about how he is living *for* yesterday instead of *in* today. When we came back, Phillip started out with an embarrassed admission that the lazy and messy issues were really small things.

> **DrL:** No, they aren't small because they *mean* something very big to you which is why you become a bastard. You're a sensitive, aware guy who can't control being a bastard. So they mean something very big for you—don't minimize them because what they mean is huge! Close your eyes, Phillip, and tell me . . . "When the house is messy, it means my wife————"
>
> **Phillip:** Doesn't care how I feel.
>
> **DrL:** "When your daughter is not busy at something, seeming lazy, it means she————"
>
> **Phillip:** She doesn't respect me as a father figure.
>
> **DrL:** You're looking in the wrong place to get verification and proof that you're a man and that you're your wife's man. When the house is neat you feel less anxious, but you really don't feel more loved—you can't convince me of that, Phillip.
>
> **Phillip:** How do I feel more loved?
>
> **DrL:** Close your eyes right now and imagine her looking up at you with adoration—you know that look from her—you've seen it. Can you see that look?
>
> **Phillip:** Okay, I see it.
>
> **DrL:** Do you like it? Does it make you feel good? Does it bring the anxiety level down?
>
> **Phillip:** Yeah.

DrL: Then when your anxiety level is up and you're needing that "fix," do what you know will bring that look to her face and then bathe in it! Neat house; anxiety down and love down. Adoring look on wife's face; anxiety down and love up. Win—win. Stop looking at the order of the house and start looking at her face. When your house is a mess and you walk in and get the anxious feeling—GASP!—walk over, lift your wife off the ground, and give her big smoochies; tell her how gorgeous she looks and that she's a hot babe and you will get the look that you need. That's what you do instead of saying something about the mess. Your mother's house is in that mess. Your house is in your wife's face. Do you understand that?

The very next day, Jolene, identifying with Phillip's situation, wrote an incredible letter to me. I am sure she represents many who saw themselves in Phillip's struggles and gained the strength to go after their needs in more constructive and productive ways.

> "I was listening to your last caller who treats his wife and daughter badly when the house is a mess. I had to stop what I was doing to hear what you had to say because I treat my family the same.
>
> "When you told him to search for the love and respect in his wife's face, the faces of my husband and loving boys came to me and brought me to tears. I have four wonderful men in my life who adore me and I treat them poorly when things are not done my way.
>
> "When you told Phillip about the house no longer being his mother's, but his wife's, you made me realize what valuable

time I have wasted on being a control freak, and how I have made myself viewed as the 'jerk' in my home. How could my family love and adore me after the way I have treated them?

"I will go home tonight, and if my house is a mess and the kids are being lazy, my reaction will be that of hugs and kisses, knowing how lucky I am to have such a wonderful family who still adore me after my bad, bad, bad behaviors.

"You made me see something that I had no idea I was doing and I thank you for that. I now have a chance to make things right.

"I'm going to change starting today and I'm going to tell my husband what a sexy stud he is and pull out a chair and have a glass of wine and look at his face, not the house."

Controlling behaviors really have nothing to do with maintaining order. Controlling behaviors are about trying to feel lovable. Unfortunately as beautifully illustrated by Phillip, controlling behaviors only empower yesterday's pain, rage, and fears to push aside today's love; ironically, the opposite is created.

Katie called me because she constantly asks her husband if/how much he loves her. She'd like to stop this behavior and offered up her own self-analysis of why she is stuck in this annoying habit of nagging her husband to give her the feedback she needs.

She began the call by telling me that she grew up feeling that her dad hated her.

Katie: My mother, even from the time I was six months old, thought that my dad hated me and that it had something to do with jealousy over me taking her time away from him . . . whatever. My relationship with my dad is a lot better now and we talk occasionally.

I've grown up feeling that I'm just inadequate, like I have issues with self-esteem that I've been working on my entire life.

She describes being married for two years to a wonderful man and that most of the time everything is fine, but sometimes, usually close to "that time of the month," she just has a hard time believing how much he loves her and just accepting what he has to say. So she badgers him with "Do you love me?" and "How much do you love me?"

What I didn't bring up at the time, but will discuss here and now, is that her father was probably never "hateful" of her; he more likely was resentful that his wife paid him no attention once she gave birth. I was frankly angrier in my mind about her mother asserting that the object of his anger was her own child and not herself! This was most likely a marital issue and not a rejection of a daughter by her father.

I did not want to bring this up during her call as I was concerned about orphaning her by yanking her illusions of her mother out from under her. Plus I don't believe that needed to be dealt with in order to make progress!

DrL: Well, Katie, nobody in the world but you can control your mouth. There is no trick. There is no magic. There is only you saying, "I choose not to drive my man nuts!"

Truth is, he's not going to love you because you're needy; he's going to love you if you're loving. So every time you feel concerned that you're not loved, act in a loving manner and create that love feeling in the other person. In other words, if you're suddenly going into your "poor me, I'm not lovable and you have to prove to me I am and make me feel good and I have to be the center of the universe and none of your feelings matter because you're just here to make me feel good" behaviors, he's bound to get very tired of it and you.

If in his mind coming home means there's an irritating little girl who is demanding and pouty, he's not even going to want to come home at some point.

If you want to know that you're loved, love the hell out of him and you'll see that love reflected back multifold.

Katie: But how do I stop needing so much?

DrL: You probably won't ever be free of those anxiety-driven impulses to squeeze instant adoration out of him. However take that impulse as narcissistic as it is, and turn it into loving generosity. You will find that two things will happen: first, giving feels good and makes one feel special to be able to bring happiness to another, and second, his response of appreciation and affection will be true and real—not extorted.

We don't ever truly *get* by grabbing, demanding, and manipulating. When we "get" that way, we know it's synthetic and we're never satisfied with a fake meal. When we see our efforts being genuinely and spontaneously rewarded, well, plan to get fat on that!

Some people sadly find it extremely difficult to get out of themselves, their neurotic, self-centered drives, and be giving. These people stay frustrated and bitter and they cause a lot of pain.

I had such a caller. This woman called to tell me that her forty-something-year-old husband is under a lot of stress because his father is going on trial for his sexual abuse of him when he was a boy. I thought she was going to ask me about how she could help him; WRONG! She called because she was miffed that he wasn't being sexual and affectionate with her, they weren't "connecting" and she needed that to feel loved. When I tried to point out that this was not the time for "getting," she tried to bury me in sad stories about her childhood and how much she needed, needed, needed . . . well, you get it.

> **DrL:** Well, there are times in our lives that we can't indulge ourselves in our own pain because WE ARE NEEDED. It is a blessing to be needed and a special kind of obligation that saves us from our own inner demons and turns us into a force for benevolence.
>
> The attitude I am trying to convey to you is that your needs don't matter right now. Just be sensitive and not demanding. Touch his face, shoulder, and arms with understanding affection. Listen without comment. Take walks. Connecting to you seems to mean that he does something to you. How 'bout you connect to him by becoming his support.

Well, that very night I got an e-mail from her expressing her disappointment in my not helping her and a long dissertation about her ugly childhood.

I couldn't get her to see, understand, and accept that sometimes we just put ourselves in a pocket in order to give our beloved air to breathe.

Barbara, another listener, wrote me the next day:

"Prior to becoming a Dr. Laura listener a few years ago, I sounded just like that caller. My husband was rarely interested in sex and never instigated physical contact, and like the caller's husband he'd been sexually abused as a child.

"I knew this entering into our marriage, yet I still pouted and moped and behaved passive-aggressively because I wasn't getting what I wanted. Also, like the caller, I felt I had ISSUES with sex because I wanted to be found attractive and validated and inundated with intimacy . . . wah . . . wah . . . wah! After listing to your program and evaluating my own behaviors, I was able to realize what a selfish baby I had been. I expected my husband to put aside all those feelings of pain and hurt which are unimaginable just because I didn't feel 'pretty.'

"Needless to say, I gave myself a swift kick in the pants (not easy to do, I might add) and started to love my husband and love my family more than I love my ISSUES.

"In return for this, I've been rewarded with a generous, forgiving, supportive husband. I've discovered the closeness of back rubs and cuddling and welcome-home hugs. Because my husband loves me, he has sex more often than he'd like, and because I love him, I have sex less often than I'd like—and that's okay. I wouldn't give the rest of it up for all the gigolos in Europe!

"Thanks for helping me enjoy what I have. With my new outlook I won't waste any more of our years together."

"Enjoy what I have." That concept is the basis of the Tenth Commandment against coveting. When we envy others for what they have, when we spend time on regrets and disappointments for what we don't have, we ensure a lack of pleasure in life. Postponing happiness until "all your ducks are in order" means never because life is not that clean, fair, or predictable. It isn't what happens to you that defines your life, it is what you do with it that does.

And if what you do with the "slings and arrows of outrageous fortune" is to pout or lash out, happiness will elude you. Leslie, a listener, wrote in response to a call she heard on my program in which a couple were fighting over the fact that the wife puttied in some holes in the wall when the husband said he would do it but didn't get to it. Leslie wrote that early in her marriage she was just like that. She and her husband would argue at the drop of a hat.

> *"In retrospect, it was never the subject, just the ability to get mad at each other over something. One day I talked to my mom about it. She and my dad had a marriage of 45 years and going strong. She said, 'Let the little things go. Let it roll off you and be grateful for your love and friendship.'*
>
> *"It seemed like such simple advice. I wasn't very good at first, but then I started realizing that I wasn't being grateful for our marriage—I was using it as a punching bag to get out a lot of stress from work, commuting, and taking care of children."*

It was insightful of Leslie to realize she was "kicking the dog," in other words, using the blessing of the intimacy and its promised safety to unleash her frustrations; frustrations she wouldn't dare take out on anyone but her dear husband for fear of being judged and dumped.

We all have those moments of "losing it," because that too is a part of real life. However if this behavior is continuous and not overwhelmed by feelings and actions of gratitude, a disaster called divorce or affair may likely result.

Pounding on your spouse because of inner frustrations does seem to be a familiar behavior, doesn't it? Annie called my program whining and complaining about how her husband doesn't realize and appreciate *how much she gave up and sacrificed.*

> **Annie:** I got pregnant at eighteen and two years later is when I married the baby's father and now we have a two-year-old. The problem is that we've been arguing a lot lately. It's just that I stay at home and because I was so young when I had our first son sometimes I don't think my husband realizes how much I gave up and how much I sacrificed.
>
> **DrL:** Didn't he sacrifice also? I don't know that you realize how much he gave up and sacrificed to be sole support of four people. Maybe he's at work thinking, "She doesn't appreciate all I'm doing for the whole family!"
>
> When one or both in a marriage starts thinking like that I know the marriage is in serious trouble. Because then it isn't about a team with different positions on that team with each taking responsibility for their own position and appreciating the other's work.
>
> And whatever you sacrificed is not his responsibility—it's yours! You had a choice: "Let's see, I'll be a brain surgeon or I'll have unprotected sex with my boyfriend. Surgeon, out-of-wedlock sex, surgeon, out-of-wedlock sex . . ." And you picked sex! You did that—you weren't raped, right? Marriage is where you love and adore someone; you sacrifice for them, and you do everything you can to make them happy.

Annie then went immediately into a litany of the "small stuff" like "he doesn't pick up his plate from the table and he relaxes with computer poker a while after work." I reminded her that her job is the home, his job is the support. Frankly—and I know this gets people worked up—women need to stop denigrating their own roles as homemakers. When a woman cleans up the dinner dishes, it is not slavery, it is being responsible and good at "her obligations." I often ask women who complain about their men not doing the laundry if they drop everything and rush to their husband's work during the day to do the filing or take the meetings. Of course they say, "No." "Then," I follow up, "why do you expect him to do your work?"

Husbands generally do the lawns, fix the cars, and work on the heavy jobs in the home. This argument that a husband should be doing his own dishes emanates from a mentality that disrespects domesticity. No one, husband included, should disrespect domesticity. Without a home running smoothly, lives within it don't run smoothly.

And as far as his doing computer poker, everyone needs brain candy time. Annie's husband's brain candy time would probably be lessened by his being greeted with more loving enthusiasm when he comes home.

Jenny, another listener, wrote that she learned the value of plain everyday loving seduction "after reading *The Proper Care and Feeding of Husbands.*" Her complaint was that she cried and begged for him to be like he was when they were dating—to woo and court her. He would always say that he'd try to do better but Mother's Day was just a store-bought card. She wrote him a three-page letter once again bemoaning her sad state. Included in this letter was her admission that she felt in competition with their three-and-a-half-year-old daughter. When on a recent business trip he mailed his daughter a toy of a father and daughter and sent

Jenny a card. When they went out to dinner, he suggested purchasing some little gift for their oldest daughter.

> *"From this suggestion of his I knew that my husband was
> capable of thinking of others and doing things to demonstrate
> his love. While reading your book, it dawned on me. Sarah
> has been demonstrating for me what I, as a wife, needed to be
> doing. The moment he walks in the door after work, she runs
> to him yelling, 'Daddy!!' and nothing else matters to her but
> that he is home.*
>
> *"I on the other hand, am too busy getting dinner ready and
> am irritated that he would actually expect me to drop what I am
> doing to give him a king's welcome. I shed many tears thinking
> about this, knowing it was not too late to start."*

She made some simple rules for herself:

1. *Stop whatever it is that I am doing and greet him.*
2. *Do my laundry, dishes, etc., during the day, and put everything away. It doesn't have to be perfect, like I want it to
   be—he just wants a comfy home to come to with a loving
   wife and children.*
3. *Just love and appreciate him without nagging and criticisms
   for the way the baby's diaper is on, or that he picked out the
   wrong pajamas.*

Evidently this worked very well. Let's hear it for priming
the pump. If you want water out of a pump, you have to prime
it *with* water to make it work!

Sometimes in addition to priming, the pump needs a smack
aside the spout! Amy's husband got such a smack while listening to my radio program. Amy generally comes home from

work and hops into the shower to calm down and relax and think about her day. She often asked him to join her, but his typical response was "But I already took a shower this morning." Perhaps he didn't fully understand the invitation or he's the type who tends to be a bit too pragmatic and thought only of hygiene.

> *"Anyways, when I came home yesterday from work, I gave him a kiss and went to take my shower when he stopped me and said, 'Can I take a shower with you . . . and would you like a glass of wine?' My eyes gleamed and then he told me about what he heard on your show, about how taking a shower together creates a good moment to talk about the day and relax TOGETHER. It was wonderful . . . and I will assume you can guess what happened next! ☺"*

I work very hard trying to give people what they deeply want, and that is to be happy. The main reason feelings of happiness are so elusive to many is that they don't really know what it is, and usually try to go about it backward. So of course when a husband or wife isn't happy the typical assumption is that it's *because* of some (imagined or exaggerated) fault of their spouse; this justifies leaving because, after all, isn't everybody entitled to be happy? But at what expense?

I had a caller, Michelle, who called to get validation for dumping her husband of three years. One hitch though—she's just discovered she's pregnant.

Michelle: I'm thirty-six. The pregnancy actually took place completely by surprise. Due to some reasons I wasn't quite happy with the marriage and I was thinking about leaving.

DrL: Well, you've got to rethink that because you now have a child who dearly needs a family structure with mom and dad. What's so bad in your marriage that you gave a thought to leaving . . . considering it's been good enough to have repeated unprotected sex and create new life.

Michelle: Right (laughs). I guess two things. One is that my husband is much older than I am.

DrL: You already knew that one when you married.

Michelle: From the financial perspective I have concerns because he's probably into getting retirement pretty soon.

DrL: Well then you might have to live modestly, but at least your child will live in a home with a mom and a dad modestly. Those are not reasons to leave and those are not reasons to destroy a child's home.

Michelle: (laughing) I guess so (pause). Yeah, um, I guess, um, another thing is I'd like to see if you have any insights into what's the best thing I can do to make the most out of the pregnancy and being happy and enjoy the whole process.

DrL: It's your moral obligation to be happy.

Michelle: Okay.

DrL: Don't you think that's everybody's moral obligation? To work as hard as they can to be happy? Or do you think everybody should be free to walk around mopey and ticked off, depressed and negative? What kind of families, communities, and societies would we have if people allowed themselves the privilege of sinking into every negative emotion they have rather than believing that they have a moral obligation to be their best selves?

I don't care if you wanted a daddy so you married an old dude. You married him and you made a kid with him. I don't care if you're not going to live in the lap of luxury because the most important thing to the child is not how much money you have, it's how loving the home is. You're bringing forth new life into the world and you're having an opportunity to live for somebody besides yourself. One of the positive reasons to have children is to learn not to be selfish anymore.

I was frankly pretty sure that I didn't reach her at all. A number of folks responded with e-mails, having identified with that caller's issue. JoAnne wrote:

"The caller sounded shocked to hear that she had a moral obligation to be happy. I currently suffer from depression and several doctors want to put me on medication. Listening to your program, having a wonderful husband and good friends has given me the strength to do it on my own.

"My prescription to myself is to get more exercise and watch what I eat. I have also started volunteering for special needs kids. I do not deny that there are days where I just want to give up—but by stepping outside of myself and doing for others, it has helped me. Not only have I been happier, but my husband has been happier. He comes with me when I exercise and cheers me on! What a wonderful MAN!

"I hope more people will take more responsibility with their attitude and do as you suggest: exercise, eat right, volunteer, and always show respect and love for those around you."

For way too many married people, their spouse is to be the antidote for all their present and past emotional aches and pains, disappointments, fears, confusions, and rage. There are at least two categories of this misplaced responsibility: one is taking past frustrations out on one's spouse as a safer and present target, the second is to try to have a second chance at a childhood by re-creating in actuality and in your mind the same circumstances as your childhood; in this way you hope to redo and then rewrite your past—and then be healed, or get revenge, or have it work out in your favor, and so forth.

Mary was raped when she was a virgin at twenty years of age. Her father did not let her prosecute the rapist. Here she is a married adult woman who "doesn't have a healthy attitude toward sex" even after seventeen years of marriage. In the first of two calls I had with Mary, I told her that she was actually quite angry with her dad for not letting her get justice.

> *Mary:* And that really upset me because I've always thought very highly of my father. I've always felt he was the only one in my family that loved me—and to hear something like that . . . and to acknowledge the truth of that . . . it hurts.

> *DrL:* Of course it does. That was what we call denial. You didn't have many supportive, loving family members in your life so you didn't want to lose your dad; which you would have had to do if you looked at the truth of the matter.

> *Mary:* Well, you told me that I should think about justice, justifiable anger, justice with the wrong man and then also about me not being able to enjoy, as you said, my God-given sensuality. And then also this past

weekend I allowed myself to enjoy sex with my husband for the first time. It was very pleasant. However I just feel angry still. Like you said I would. I still feel angry.

DrL: I want you to continue to feel anger where anger is due; but it isn't due to your husband and it isn't due to your sex life. You can stay angry for the rest of your life, it's okay—it is valid anger. Picture having a coat with two pockets. You need to have anger in one pocket—anger toward your dad not permitting justice—and your marriage and sensuality in another pocket. Right now you have them commingled. I'm just asking you to separate them out.

You are not getting justice with respect to the guy who raped you or your dad who wanted to keep it quiet. You're certainly not getting justice by spending the rest of your life not enjoying your sensuality. You're not getting justice by punishing your husband for the rapist and your dad!

So since you're failing at your task of getting justice by denying yourself pleasure with your husband and by whitewashing good ole dad, it all seems like that's something you ought to stop doing.

You'll never get justice for what happened. You have to accept that. There will never be justice. So keep the anger in your left pocket, and put your sensuality and your love for your husband in your right pocket. It's going to be a while before your attitude switches over. Keep your rage if you wish, but keep it in the left pocket . . . and don't visit it often.

What we can learn from Mary's situation is that the past has tentacles that squeeze the life out of today when we have *unresolved* passionate hurts and disappointments. One of the toughest things to do is look at the past *objectively* when there are simply truths we don't want to know. In Mary's case, the truths were that it was too late to get justice for the rape, and that her father didn't want to be embarrassed and therefore was not her protector. Since she hid herself from these truths, the tentacles followed her into her marriage. Her "resolution" to these problems was to punish her husband for the sins of her father and rapist. What she gained by slicing those tentacles was the freedom to be a woman in love *in spite* of losing the fantasies of a perfect father and justice.

Probably the primary childhood issue, whether or not there was abuse or outright negligence, is the feeling of not having been important to your parents, and not getting the attention and tender loving care all children crave and require. The end result of all this loss is sometimes an overfocus on being sad. What does "sad" create? It creates lots of attention and care-taking coming *in* with minimal responsibility going *out* to others. This is like being the squeaky wheel or the noisy kid who gets all the attention.

Obviously this kind of behavior from a spouse is draining to the marriage and the family. Recently a caller talked about how she could not stop bad memories from her childhood from filling her every minute and she was just wrecking her life. By the end of the call, I made it clear to her that she was not letting go of the bad memories because being *in pain* all the time gave her control over her family; she forced them into showing her attention, taking care of her, and, like any child, she was not responsible for giving.

The result of this call was a virtual avalanche of e-mail and faxes as so many people recognized themselves in the caller, or recognized themselves as the victim of such a spouse.

Rachel, a listener, wrote:

"You had a call on Monday that changed my life. I have tears in my eyes as I write this—tears of relief at finally understanding a certain behavior and tears of relief because now I know how to fix it.

"I was born into a chaotic household where the adults looked to the children to have their needs met (emotional and otherwise) and burdened the children with adult matters (money woes, in-law problems, job stress).

"I was the oldest girl and was assigned the mommy/caretaking role from a very young age. I never in my life felt like someone cared for me the way a parent should care for a child.

"Your caller got anxious and worried about her life, and then allowed her anxiety to debilitate and paralyze her so that she felt unable to do something as simple as housework or cook dinner, much less give her children and husband some emotional support, help with homework, or spare a kind word for them at the end of the day.

"She never had anyone really take care of her as a child either, and whenever she got anxious, she shut down so that someone else (her husband) would be forced to take over her responsibilities.

"Hearing you tell her that this was why she acted as she did changed my life. For the first time I have an inkling of what drives my anxiety. I use anxiety as a time machine to try and go back to the past, turn into a child, and have someone else take care of me and my problems! WOW. WOW.

"The long-term challenge for me will be to reset my thinking so that when I feel that old worry and anxiety stirring up in me, I don't take it as a signal to shut down and see if I can get my husband to parent me. Now when I feel worry and anxiety,

that will be a signal to take a positive ADULT action: kiss and hug someone I love, clip some coupons, take a walk, clean out a closet—do something productive that HELPS my life in some small way."

How incredible that Rachel and so many other listeners were willing to embrace such a truth without shame, defensiveness, and denial. To realize and own that you're wasting precious adult time, when you could finally enjoy loving and being loved, needing and being needed, focusing only on the getting because you didn't get enough when you were a child is of course sad—but truth sets you free, if you embrace it.

If you don't, then this letter will be about you! Greg, a listener, also responded to that call:

"I was listening to your radio show recently and heard the caller who kept dwelling on her past in order to get attention and care from her husband. I recently ended a relationship with a woman who also had a troubled past. For the first thirteen years of her life she had a father who was a drug dealer and a mother who abused her. Eventually she ended up in foster care until she was eighteen.

"Throughout our relationship whatever I did for her was never enough. I was constantly accused of being selfish and uncaring. For the first year I believed these accusations and continually tried harder to please her, comfort her, and make her happy.

"I then began listening to your show and began to recognize what was really going on. I was trying to rescue a damsel in distress—only to end up with a distressed damsel! The more I gave, the more she wanted and the worse the manipulations, such as crying and putting me down, became.

"I continually hoped that one day she would realize what she was doing and recognize that I really do care about her. That never happened."

Fortunately many callers and listeners get it, embrace it, and change. Interestingly, some spouses don't turn to their spouse for the parent replacement job. Sometimes they go straight elsewhere.

Steve called ostensibly about him not living up to his full potential because he did "bad things" to protect his brother from his mother's wrath. Rumor had it that Steve's brother may have been the product of some affair of his mother's.

DrL: So your mother may have had a child by some other guy, your father stayed, but then she was unkind to the child.

Steve: Yeah, kind of punishing him for some problems. At the time, of course, growing up and even as teenagers, we had no idea why one of us might be treated bad and the other one not.

DrL: What can I help you with today?

Steve: Well, as kids, he was treated badly and I think I've kind of slipped into a pattern of being a huge trial to my parents to try to get some of the negative off of him and focused on me maybe.

DrL: So you're thinking that you sacrificed some well-being in order to protect him?

Steve: Yeah, I did just about everything wrong I could think of.

I then asked Steve to close his eyes and revisit his childhood without his brother in the picture at all. I directed him to give me some other reason he might want to stick it to his mother by driving her nutsy with bad things he'd done. Steve's response was an incredibly heavy sigh, after which he described her as very emotionally unavailable and distant. His teachers all the way through school had informed Steve's parents that he was gifted.

> **DrL:** So you were mad at her and didn't fulfill your potential. Is that what you're saying? Keep your eyes closed . . .
>
> **Steve:** Yeah. I mean she expected everything . . .
>
> **DrL:** How did your brother benefit?
>
> **Steve:** In the long run, a lot; he's been hugely successful because she gave him nothing and so he bent over backward to prove that he could do what she said he couldn't.
>
> **DrL:** Perhaps some of your actions were intended to protect your brother by taking the heat off him—but I think it's more that since your mother's love seemed so conditional you didn't give her the conditions!
>
> **Steve:** That makes sense.
>
> **DrL:** How does that relate to what you're doing today? Do you love your children? Do they know it? Do you love your wife? Does she know it?
>
> **Steve** (holding back tears): It's just hard to be close.

I told Steve that it was sad that he was just like his mother. I asked him to tell me about the future when his kids were going to call and tell me how they're struggling with life because their dad was so cold and distant. Interestingly, he offered up immediately that it would be one over the other who would make that call.

DrL: How does your boy, Ben, make you feel better about yourself? In one sentence, "He makes me feel better about myself because he————"

Steve: Because he's bubbly and always happy no matter what I do. He's always excited when I come home.

DrL: So—you've made him your mother!!

Steve: I guess I look to him for emotional support.

DrL: You don't get close to your wife or kids, and you have one kid living to please you and make you feel good. Meanwhile, you give nothing to them. Isn't it amazing that the thing you wanted the most from your mother—

Steve: Is the thing I'm withholding from everyone else.

DrL: And you won't let yourself have. That which you are squeezing from your boy, you need to get from your woman. Your woman's got to be the one human being on the face of the earth you feel safe being vulnerable with.

He went on to describe being afraid to go to his wife for loving, attentive affection because, like his mother, she won't give it. I told him that he's really going to have to force himself to be Steve and not Stevie, a child.

"No man is going to enjoy life when he's still scrambling after his mommy or protecting himself from his mommy. You got starved by your mommy for half your life and the other half of your life you're planning to starve yourself?"

At this point I gave him his assignment before making an appointment to talk with him some two weeks later. I told him to go home, walk over to his wife, lift her off the ground, swing her around, give her a big huggy smooch, and then later when the kids are in bed to say to her, "Can I put my head in your lap and can you just pet my head because I need peace and joy?" The first part of the assignment was to tap into the Steve part; the second part was to then receive the loving support of a wife while still being a man.

Two weeks later Steve called back and told me that he did the assignment and it was fabulous.

DrL: Did you give her a big, slurpy kiss on the face?

Steve: Oh yeah—and then later in the evening she was more than willing to sit there and give me that other kind of attention. It was great and it changed my attitude about my relationship and it's really, really improved things. I'm not so concerned that she's going to reject me somehow and not give me what I didn't get when I was kid so I'm more focused on accepting what she can give me now and not accepting less than that.

DrL: Do you realize you went from zero to one hundred?

Steve: In one day pretty much. Because it's been good and much better with her that I'm sharing more and being more emotional and close with both of my kids and everything has been good.

You may sniff your nose and say that people can't change that much that fast—but you'd be wrong because a shift in attitude that opens you up to letting your husband/wife in close and personal lets the love through. When people feel loved and appreciated, the bad old stuff just doesn't seem that important. Steve, and so many men and women, are stuck because they fear that *if* they're vulnerable to their spouses, the results will be negative and there will be no hope ever for happiness. That's a risk you have to be willing to take—and most of you will have a success as warm as Steve's. Keeping on track gets easier and easier.

Jeff and Wendy called in to my program because he and Wendy had gotten into a dispute, after which she called him on the cell phone screaming that he was mean to her. Jeff said he was calling for an opinion about whether or not he's mean or if it is a communication problem.

I love that term "communication problem." Whenever I ask people to clarify that . . . they can't. I don't think that many marriages are stuck on communication problems, whatever they are. I think that most marriages are stuck on people needing or hurting so much (from their childhoods, primarily) that they forget to or resist giving love. Jeff and Wendy were no exception to that rule.

You may be interested in knowing that I was inundated with critical e-mails for two weeks after my two calls with Steve and Wendy. Everybody—save one—said I was totally wrong.

What happened was that I asked Wendy to describe one or two situations where Jeff was clearly mean. She talked about his very angry expressions, very loud voice, angry tone, and angry delivery. I wondered why expressing anger had to look friendly? She said that he would get angry too quickly at little things and that this had gotten worse over the years.

I then went to Jeff and asked him why his fuse was so short. He said that he's not getting respect from Wendy—and that this was getting worse over the years.

Chick or egg?

I asked Jeff for two examples of Wendy's disrespect. The first was when Wendy asked him to put air in the van's tires. He went and did that and after coming back, Wendy went out to look at the tires and saw that there was a screw in the tire and asked him if he'd checked for the screw and he replied that he hadn't checked the tires—he just put air in them and came home. He then goes to put the spare on and she tells him to forget it and take it to the gas station for repairs because she doesn't believe he's going to do it right. Jeff blows up.

Second example: Jeff teaches sixth grade math and science. Their son took his little volcano experiment to school and needed to bring the ingredients for it, baking soda and vinegar. Even though he himself had gone out the day before to get fresh baking soda, he grabbed the old baking soda and took it to school with his son and the volcano. Wendy was mad because he took the old baking soda. Jeff blows up.

I had Wendy hang up so that I could talk to Jeff alone. I told Jeff, in the nicest way possible, that he's just not paying attention to things that actually most guys pay a lot of attention to. I described Wendy's behaviors as a reaction to his not paying attention and not a display of disrespect. I gave him the assignment to call me back the next day without Wendy and to tell me why he chose not to pay attention and aggravate her on purpose.

The sky opened up with men e-mailing me all afternoon

and all night saying Wendy was a bitch, Jeff was within his rights to be angry, and that I was dead wrong.

When Jeff called the next day, he still fought me about following through on his assignment, which was to "think about why you *chose* to irritate her." His comeback was a repeat of yesterday's, "I can accept constructive criticism, if it is in fact constructive, and if there's something that I'm doing wrong. I know you said my examples from yesterday were poor examples."

> *DrL:* No, they were very good examples—not of Wendy being disrespectful—but of the passive-aggressive behavior that exists when a person feels tremendous hostility but has difficulty being up front about it. She called you mean; I don't think you're mean at all. But it was interesting that you gave two very good passive-aggressive examples: taking the wrong baking soda when you knew better and not bothering to check a deflating tire for a nail.

I then asked him to take me back to when he was eight (yes, I just pulled that one out of a hat).

> *DrL:* Who's in the house, and what are they doing?

> *Jeff:* Nobody is in the house and I'm not at the house either. I'm at a babysitter. A very strict lady who made us play board games. We were eight kids stuck in a fifteen-by-fifteen room.

> *DrL:* I see, so that was how she controlled a large number of children; you played board games and stayed put. This is tougher on boys than on girls.

From there Jeff, with much prodding from me, painted a picture of parents not only uninvolved with his interests, but actually negative about the things he liked. He had gotten into wrestling and his parents didn't like that because of the violence . . . the aggression. Financially they were supportive, but not emotionally.

Basically the picture I got from our lengthy discussion was that women were a big disappointment to him in particular. First, a mother who was uninvolved and freaked out about aggression in sports, and the control of a strict babysitter who kept him caged up. I suggested to Jeff that he was an angry man; anger is the final by-product of hurt. And since aggression was squelched, his hurt/anger came out as passive-aggressive. His pattern of dealing with Wendy reflects his reaction to his early upbringing. If Wendy is not lovingly supportive of something, doesn't make him feel good about himself, or seems to control him, he strikes back with passive-aggressive behaviors. It is when he is "called" on this behavior that he loses it more directly.

So-called communication problems are generally that we're not talking about the current moment; the current moment is just a trigger for a memory. And Jeff's memory, as I told his wife, Wendy, the next day, is filled with not being supported, being abandoned, being controlled in terms of his natural male-child energy and aggression, instead of hearing a lot of hoorays and "You're terrific—we think you're great," and "We love you," and "We're here."

Wendy responded with, "And she continues to do that to this day."

I left Jeff with a deeper understanding that he was overreacting to perceived slights from Wendy because he was already primed to believe that she was "just another controlling, emotionally uninvolved, and nonsupportive woman." Interestingly, when I posed that to him, he responded by telling me how wonderful she was. And, from my discussions with her, she was indeed wonderful and loving. I suggested to Jeff that he behave toward Wendy as though he actually believed that instead of trying to punish her. I suggested to Wendy that she be aware of opportunities to support his ego by compliments and by giving him the respect of expecting him to do the right thing—without motherly follow-through.

It is not an unusual concept to imagine that a man might be unpleasant with his wife because he had problems with a mom; it is a little less obvious to imagine he wouldn't have sex with his wife because he had problems with a father.

Kenny and Lynn, married four years (her third, his first) called because Lynn felt very rejected sexually. She expressed loving him because he was a good and honest man for whom she has great admiration and respect. Kenny described himself as never feeling he had the competence that he could take care of a wife and children and give them the life they deserved.

> **DrL:** What do you think drove you to that conclusion about yourself?
>
> **Kenny:** From my father and my mother. My father was an alcoholic and terrorized our house. I was always just a coward in the corner and had fear of him and everything. My mother didn't protect me.
>
> **DrL:** When did you stop having fear?
>
> **Kenny:** I still have fear. I just deal with it a lot better now.

After interviewing Lynn a bit more, I learned that they didn't have sexual intimacy before marriage either.

DrL: Kenny, you didn't marry to have a man-woman relationship. You really married to not be alone and have some womanly-motherly companionship. Isn't that right? Lynn married to have a husband and you married to have a mom.

Kenny (wistfully): A mom I never had. Well, what do we do now?

DrL: I guess you're at a crossroads. Here you are almost half a century old and the rest of your life is going to be a shorter amount of time than what you've had up till now. So, Kenny, you need to decide whether you're going to continue being the damaged little boy or a man with his own woman. You have a decision to make, sir. Do you want to be a man for the rest of your life or do you want to continue being the hungry little boy?

Kenny: I want to be a man.

DrL: Then say in a loud, firm, grown-man voice—instead of that little boy whisper—"I can be a MAN!"

Kenny: I CAN BE A MAN!

DrL: Right! Your parents robbed you of a childhood. Don't let how they were rob you of your manhood.

I asked them to call back in one week. When they did, the transformation was amazing for both of them.

Kenny: Last week you helped me learn that I was a child of an abusive drunk and that I was robbed of a normal childhood. I continued to rob myself of a normal adulthood. It's true. I believe within myself there's been a shy, scared little boy for a long time. Your assignment was for me to think about what it means to be a married man. This was difficult for me. The first thing that came to mind is that I can't live within myself as a married man because there's someone who depends on me to give of myself. Even though I feel the fear and self-doubt, I can't live within myself and be a married man. I have to intellectually or somehow come out of that and understand that even through the fear I have to act otherwise.

You pointed out some little things, that I spoke like a child, for example. So I've been trying to speak more clearly and firmly and let her know that I'm a confident man and that she's safe with me as her man. That's one thing. I've been trying to show her that I love her and that she is the only woman for me; that I adore her. I'm trying to come out of myself a little at a time. It's really hard to do.

Lynn opened up to explain her feelings too.

Lynn: My reaction to all of this since yesterday is a lot of hurt. I know that sounds bad, but I had never considered that he had married me for a mother. Although it explained a lot of our past before and during marriage because he is always telling me what a wonderful mother I am [she has four adult children from one of her marriages]. I love to be told I'm a good mother, but I'd rather be told that I'm a beautiful woman by Kenny.

Lynn wrote to me several days after our second conversation:

> *"I saw a tremendous change in him throughout the week you gave him to think about what it means to be a married man and I continue to see great changes. I have no doubt anymore that he is MY MAN as I am HIS WOMAN. I would like to thank you from the very depths of my soul for your help and guidance in Kenny's life as well as my own. One man and his woman—my dream as well as his—came true.*

This sad scenario, marrying for a parent and not a spouse, is not unusual, but is usually the last thing either imagines. Jan, a listener, wrote:

> *"Your comments to the woman who wanted her husband to be her daddy haunted me. When you asked her to say something great about her husband, and she said only that he was incredibly supportive, you interpreted that to mean that she was looking only to be taken care of and that she wasn't treating her husband like HER MAN. Wow, did that ever hit home.*
>
> *"I never realized that I was doing that to my husband, but after hearing your comments, I began to list in my mind all of the ways that I try to make my husband my dad instead of my man.*
>
> *"This insight led me further down that road, and I realized that if I wanted him to parent me, then I must want to stay a little girl. Then I began to think of all the ways I act like a girl instead of a grown woman. In spite of all my degrees, children, and 23-year marriage, I feel like a scared little girl inside— always fearing that someday someone will find me out for the imposter that I am. I don't take care of myself physically like I*

should, my house is disorganized, I feel out of control 99% of the time—like I could fall apart any minute from the weight of acting like an adult.

"I decided that whenever I want to act like that little girl and feel entitled, fearful, stubborn, or demanding, I am going to choose to act like a mature woman instead. What that is exactly, I don't always know—but I'm going to try to find out."

It is not always that being "starved" emotionally as a child results in demanding good parenting from a spouse. Sometimes it means that the hungry adult-child starves out their spouse because their unfamiliarity and discomfort with affection scares them. They've spent all their lives surviving without it—opening up to affection becomes a very frightening risk.

I told one such caller, Maria, to "sit down with your husband, hold his hand, look straight into his eyes and say, 'You are a wonderful and loving man and I'm scared of love because I never had it. Sometimes I push it away only because I'm scared of it and I'm not comfortable. So please understand that I'm not rejecting you—I love you and you're wonderful. I want to kiss you, I want to hug you, and I want to feel comfortable about it.' "

I went on to give her an assignment I described as one that would make her think I'm nuts or hate me altogether. "Maria, for one month I have an assignment for you. For one month, every day, you hug him, you kiss him, and you have sex. Every day. But *you* do it. You're in control. You're going to like this after a while. But the first week or so you're going to hate me . . . then you'll discover something—and when you discover it, call me back."

Maria called back a month later sounding, frankly, like a different woman. She admitted that I was right, she hated me for two weeks. After two weeks, she actually began looking forward to the affection and sex. She loved feeling good about him, about sex, about hugging, and about feeling close. She sounded giggly, strong, and happy.

What she discovered is that she actually had a choice to live as though today were only an extension of yesterday, or its own promise and opportunity. She discovered that talking about something is not as powerful as living it to change one's perspective. She discovered that she could be happy if she put in the determined effort. She discovered that happiness is always possible.

It's your turn to discover you no longer have to be the enemy of your current opportunity to be happy and make someone else happy.

Chapter 3

The Good, the Bad, and the Ugly

I don't know how many times I've tried to explain to callers that marriage is not advanced dating. Somebody fun to date is not necessarily someone you will be able to count on when the "going gets tough." An all too familiar caller problem has been that they partied well while dating, but after having a child, bills, and mundane, repetitive responsibilities, being married to someone who continues to party is . . . well . . . no party at all. Another typical caller complaint is that their spouse has an unacceptable point of view or behavior which they accepted while dating but is now too huge to suffer any longer.

Somehow many folks have a notion about marriage that it will automatically change everything to the positive and "their way." Disappointments occur when expectations don't meet reality; and the reality is that dating, even shacking up, are nothing like marriage at all. In "shacking up," two ambivalent people stay "two," while in marriage, two committed people become "one." This makes shacking up a bad warm-up for marriage, as statistics of higher breakup rates, domestic violence, affairs, and emotional problems demonstrate.

The question does linger in people's minds these days as to whether or not marriage truly has anything to offer them that being single or shacking up doesn't already satisfy. In one of my many surveys in preparation for this book, I asked listeners (male and female separately) a number of questions in order to answer that question.

MARRIAGE

1. What was your biggest surprise to learn about marriage?
2. In what way(s) has marriage made you a better person?
3. What are the benefits of being married vs. single?

Below are *typical* answers from women:

1. What was your biggest surprise to learn about marriage?

- "Having to let go of the notion that everything can be compromised—sometimes on an issue either me or my husband will not get their own way, and I've learned that's okay because we can't be satisfied all of the time."
- "That I have this immense power to either ruin my husband's and children's lives, or enrich them. If I decide to disrespect my husband, then my children will disrespect their father as well. My mood, and to what degree I allow that mood to dictate my behavior, has a direct result on everyone else's mood, and therefore, their daily lives. Amazing! And scary! And so very humbling."

- "After I said my vows on my wedding day I felt even more committed and bound to my husband, even though we had dated monogamously and felt committed for a long courtship."
- "That marriage didn't solve all of my problems and it didn't make me feel complete. What a letdown."
- "Because my parents were divorced, the biggest surprise I had was how harmonious marriage could be. I expected that fighting and acrimony were just part of marriage . . . but that's not so!"
- "That I couldn't just think about 'me' anymore; there was another human being to consider in every single decision. Sounds obvious, but it's not!"
- "That there is always more learning and maturing to do."
- "I never really knew how much work (bills, meals, cleaning, kids, family stuff, emotions, problems to solve) it took to have a happy, well-working marriage. It takes responsibility and accountability." "It takes more than love to get through this life together." "That marriage is a business partnership as much as it is a romance. You have to manage your life together—your money, children, home, work, relatives, etc."
- "I was most surprised to learn how dull and exciting marriage actually is. We have basically been doing the same thing every day for the past twenty-one years—but each day still seems exciting while we're living it . . . marriage has a way of making life more fun, in an ordinary way."
- "That you could love someone so strongly one minute and want to kill them the next minute." "That people are like coins; there are two sides to a coin and you cannot

separate them. The side of the coin you love, is linked to a side you do not love and can drive you crazy."

- "I was surprised to vividly experience the difference between men and women. My husband is a wonderful man, but he is not concerned about housekeeping or making social plans. I think to make marriage work, men and women need to respect their gender differences and personality differences."
- "How amazing it is to *belong* to somebody."
- "Was learning that the 'in love' feelings fade. But an even bigger surprise was finding out that if you stay faithful, honor your commitment, and keep doing the right thing, those feelings are replaced with something far deeper and precious than the dating feelings ever could be."

The single most common response had to do with every day not being full of butterflies and passionate kisses. This means that an obvious motivation to be giving, patient, and loyal, those lovey-dovey feelings, come and go. This means that it takes work to stay committed.

Jake, a recent caller, has been married only four years, and has two children, three and one. He told me that about a year ago their "closeness was unraveling." He began an affair some nine months ago, which ended recently because the "honey" was angry about him not spending enough time with her. (Sidebar: I couldn't stop laughing when he said this because it seems odd that a woman who wants a lot of "intimacy" would pick a man with a wife and two very small children!) I resisted giving him hell about his affair because he already presented himself as truly remorseful; additionally, with the time I have available for a call, I wanted to focus more on keeping this family together.

I asked him what "unraveling" meant and he responded that daily life just got repetitive and boring and this affair put excitement into his life again. I told him that when one spouse is bor*ed* it is usually because they are bor*ing*. Expecting some automatic magic to transform you from the tired and stressed human being you are at the end of a workday (homemaking or employee status) into a happy and carefree individual is going to result in disappointment and resentment.

Consider coming together with your spouse at the end of the day as an opportunity to drink from a well. The water doesn't come up out of the well by its own force; *you* actually have *to do* something active to get the water to soothe your parched lips. The same goes for psyches. When at the end of the day you yearn for some relief from the day, prepare your mind and heart the same way you'd prepare for anything else:

- Start thinking positively about it (think *good* thoughts about your spouse and warm thoughts about the family together at day's end).

- Get ready in your mind something you're going to say to be fresh water to your spouse's parched being.

- Package up your problems and day's annoyances and put them on the floor in the back of your basement closet; don't compete with each other's day by having the worst story of the day's problems.

- Be affectionate in small ways; a touch, a kiss on the cheek, an offering of a flower (and this all goes *two* ways), a suggestion that the other relax while you do something nice for them like get an ice tea, etc.

- Find something special about that day to compliment him/her on.

- Invite your spouse to have an opinion on something you're dealing with . . . and *do not* criticize their response—instead, be gracious and grateful.

- Ask him/her something specific concerning something you know they had to deal with today . . . and look interested even if you're not!

The key is to give, give, and give some more. Coming out of me, me, me is the sure way to reduce your own tension and to get the best from your spouse; their appreciation will turn into loving, considerate behavior toward you, and the well will gush and satisfy you more than any nagging or demanding could ever.

When you are planning for making someone else happy, and when you are using your beloved's mere existence to enrich you, you can *never* be bored!

2. In what way(s) has marriage made you a better person?

- "By showing me that putting someone else's needs *before* my own is the true definition of happiness."
- "More honest, because I have someone who holds me accountable; more responsible, because my actions affect him; more relaxed because I know I have someone who cares; more confident, because I know he loves me as I am—and that alone gives me strength."
- "Being with him makes me want to be a better person."
- "I have felt accepted and loved for exactly who I am, the good and the bad, and therefore have been able to accept

my husband and our kids in the same way. I used to seek an impossible goal of perfection for myself and others and I was miserable, always falling short."

- "He is the logical one, and if I actually sit long enough and listen to and follow his counsel, it is actually good advice. We complement each other; I am the emotional one. So where I lack, he makes up for and vice versa."

- "Together we make an awesome team."

- "Learning to share, care, and love another person makes me a better person."

- "I like myself more because I see that my husband loves me."

- "My marriage taught me to be less touchy. I had to survive as a child and young adult. Now I let my husband scratch my soft underbelly and I LOVE IT!"

- "Marriage has made me a better person because my husband has taught me a whole new way to look at life. I tend to be an anxious person who gives up at the slightest frustration. My husband has brought in stability and peace, as well as teaching me perseverance. He has a great sense of humor too—so he makes me laugh."

- "I really feel like I have been given a dream partner to share life with and while that is a gift, it is also a huge responsibility. The desire I have to see my husband happy was surprisingly overwhelming for me, considering that I have always been a self-focused, depressed person (childhood scars). My problem was a need to have him parent me with daily reassurance. However I could see in his eyes from time to time, a longing for ME to truly KNOW that I was okay so that I could be his peaceful woman and not his anxious little girl. When he was tired and emotionally drained from his workday, I know the last thing he needed was for me to drain whatever drop was left in his emotional tap. That is when the accountability part kicked in: I LOVED HIM SO MUCH THAT I WOULD CHANGE. I started practicing not being in a slump all day and now it is becoming almost natural!"

I was most touched that the majority of the women's answers had to do with (1) learning not to be selfish, self-centered, and focusing on primarily "what's in it for me," and, (2) that a man and a woman *complement* each other *and* become "one." The becoming "one" issue is a controversial one in the feminist community since it implies a woman is owned or oppressed by a man and can't be her own person.

Carey, a listener, wrote that her husband of eighteen years spontaneously surprised her with a gift. Out of the blue he ordered her a new personalized license plate for the truck she uses. Her husband has an unusual name: Brud. Her new license plate says BRUDSWF (Brud's wife). Did she throw a fit and yell that she is not a possession? Nope!

> *"I felt so honored and loved when he presented me with this gift. He knows how hard I work to be a good wife to him and a good mother to our four children. He appreciates what I do and values my contribution to our satisfying marriage. I know that he is a good man and I am so proud to be known as his wife.*
>
> *"Women usually look at me with scorn and distaste when I explain what the letters mean, but men usually love it and tell me that their wives would never go for it. What a shame because I am sooo proud to be known as the wife of a kind, considerate, loving husband. Sign me: appreciative and appreciated in California."*

Tausha, another listener, had a great story to tell. For her husband's birthday she drew him a picture of a knight decked out in shiny armor, with a long, sharp sword in one hand, and a large, decorated shield in the other. The knight in her picture is actively fighting a big, ugly, fiery dragon. Overlooking this scene is a fair maiden in a tower. *"I tried to make the maiden look like me so that my husband would recognize that it was me up in the tower, and that I was anxiously watching and waiting for him, with his strength and courage, to slay that dragon and come climbing up the tower for me."*

Enclosed with her sketch was a note that read: *"You are my knight in shining armor. Thank you for putting on that heaving, binding armor each day and going out and slaying those dragons. Your bravery in defense of me and the kids is more than I could have ever hoped for. I will forever be your maiden."*

Whew! What an incredible sentiment to express. There are many out there in our society, and those reading this now, who would mock her sketch, suggesting that it implies the fair maiden was too weak, and should have just woven a ladder of her own hair, climbed down that tower on her own, and then either run far away from the violent scene, or taken the sword from the knight and accuse him of slaying the dragon the wrong way as she slayed the dragon herself. But, as Tausha continued,

"I am proud to be the maiden who works hard at home taking care of our three children, the dog, the cooking, and the cleaning. I am proud to be able to make a warm meal and a comfortable place for my husband to lie. Thank you, Dr. Laura, for instilling in me a 'maiden' attitude where I can encourage my knight to get out and fight, and then welcome him home to heal from

his battles. Words cannot express my gratitude to you for your service to women like me, who are doing their best to create peaceful palaces."

I don't know, folks, do these women really sound oppressed and depressed?

3. What are the benefits of being married vs. single?

- "I always have my best friend here with me. Sometimes we can sit and say nothing for hours, but know the love and comfort are there. We can say absolutely anything to each other without fear of being judged or unloved."
- "I have the benefit of knowing that someone loves me enough to commit himself legally to me. We're forever responsible to each other under the law and in God's eyes."
- "Knowing that no matter what difficulties life throws at us there is always someone in your corner to help you through it."
- "The benefit I have gained in being married is that there isn't a single joy or burden that I carry alone. Sharing all this makes the joys sweeter and the burdens lighter."
- "Just not having to date anymore is a big benefit—it's scary out there. The world keeps filling up with amoral, liberal morons who want sex on the first date because the women available now don't think twice about giving it to them. With the exception of church, where the heck can a decent girl go to meet a decent guy?"
- "Sharing a home and a life is amazing. I am never lonely. I never eat alone. I don't sleep alone. I always have someone to talk to, even when that talking is picking a fight—I

have someone to make up with. I have someone who respects, supports, and loves me every day."

- "Safe, happy, and fulfilling sex."
- "Being with someone who understands what I am thinking and saying."
- "Making memories with someone."
- "Married life is more secure, stable, and comfortable. Having an intimate relationship in which I can be completely vulnerable, playful, passionate, and seductive is more than I ever dreamed of having."
- "When you have someone who is willing to lay their life on the line for you AND make love to you until you are beyond satisfied . . . well, there is nothing greater than that!"
- "I get to sleep next to this adorable, loving, amazing, generous, caring, soulful, handsome, giving father to our children man for the rest of my life. If I were single, my bed would be empty—as well as my life."

Actually, I don't think I have to add anything to this selection, do I?

I am convinced, as I have said earlier and will keep repeating (!), that attitude is everything. I know from the feedback I received from the folks who contributed to these surveys, that many of them felt revitalized in their sentiments about their spouses and their marriages just by filling out the survey and massaging their thoughts around these positive marital issues/ questions. There's good and bad in every situation, however the more you review the bad, the worse you feel; the more you review the good, the better you feel. When you think more positively about life, love, and marriage, you instantly become more patient, compassionate, forgiving of the small stuff, and very grateful for what you have. This attitude shift immediately changes the marriage from a chore and a cross to bear, to a pleasure and a blessing to embrace.

Below are *typical* answers from men:

1. What was your biggest surprise to learn about marriage?

- "Your free time is cut by 80 percent."
- "The problems of my wife (with her family, etc.) become our problems."
- "I was surprised how quickly the frequency of having sex diminished."
- "That the bad times and the pain would be so remarkably awful: the agony over a sick spouse or child or the times our relationship got bad."
- "I was amazed how little my outside friends and activities mattered. I would much rather and still do rather be with my wife and do things with her."
- "How feelings fluctuate during the years; but in a solid marriage, one thing remains the same and that is that you love your spouse."
- "How destructive extended family can be."
- "Married women do not compromise much; it is left up to the man to compromise to his wife's perceived problem."
- "Keeping track of schedules, paying bills, spending money on girl things I never thought about because all I was thinking about was the sex. That was a huge adjustment for me."
- "Marriage, I learned, was an opportunity for character building. Letting go of one's opinions, desires for the good of the whole."
- "It was surprising how many decisions she makes tied into emotions rather than sound, logical basis."

- "The struggle to make needed sacrifices and having to support a family. I can't just walk away when times get tough, I need to stick through it all. Giving up of hobbies to support the family and toning down sexual drives and desires to fit more to her liking."
- "It's not just about me and I must have her approval when I am to do something."
- "How many times I'm requested to go shopping."
- "It's not easy and requires work. My parents always made it look so easy."
- "Women are more complicated than I first thought."
- "How much children impact a marriage . . . disciplining, etc."
- "The biggest surprise was how much a woman misleads her man until the ring is in place. Once the ring was set, she figured she would set the record straight as to how the structure of the relationship will be built, and it was nothing like the relationship we had talked about before we were married. It took me months to convince her that there was no master/slave clause in our vows and I would not be held hostage to emotional or sexual blackmail. Thirty-five years later and we're still going strong."
- "How different women see marriage as opposed to dating. The women's attitude to please, to meet her man's requirements seem to sag after marriage even with the best, most loyal woman. It is as though her objective as a couple changes overnight; 'We must now start building a home and family in lieu of concentrating on each other.' "
- "Sex did not become a free and easy, fun activity. It became and remains a power struggle."
- "That two *can* live as cheaply as one!"

• "My biggest surprise would have to be how my happiness is directly connected to my wife's happiness . . . and when she's not happy, I'm not happy, and I try very hard to 'fix it.' "

What stands out the most in comparing the answers from the women to these from the men, as well as reflecting on phone calls and e-mails to my program, is how dominant, in general, women are in setting the tone and style of the relationship of marriage. Men aim to please, and acquiesce to feminine direct and indirect pressure to do so, while women aim to be pleased, and generally consider this imbalance reasonable.

Women in particular like to talk about the necessity for good and open communication. Unfortunately, when a guileless man communicates simple facts, that is often enough to set off a woman's insecurities. For example, a recent female caller complained to me that her husband, a kitchen contractor, came home from a job in a private home and told her, "My goodness! The guy's wife came to the door in skimpy clothes and was acting flirtatiously." My caller was furious that he said that to her!

DrL: Let me understand the source of your anger. Was he responsible for how this woman behaved?

Caller: Well, no.

DrL: Did he take advantage of the situation and have a fling?

Caller: No, of course not.

DrL: "Of course not" means you trust him and his fidelity to you?

Caller: Yes . . . but . . .

DrL: Please, don't "but" me; you either recognize his loyalty or you don't. He can't control her behavior but he controlled his own. If that doesn't please you, what would? Furthermore, why don't you greet him at the bedroom door the same way you imagine she greeted him at her front door? Or are you going to give me the "I hate my body so he can't have some" typical female nonsense?

Caller: Okay, okay—I got it.

DrL: You only had something to fear if he didn't tell you. That would likely mean one of two things: he's taking her up on it, or he can't talk to you because of your insecurities and hypersensitivities.

As I have said probably too many times before, it is the woman who rules the relationship and the home when she's married to your typical fellow (omitting, of course, narcissists, psychopaths, and addicts). That is the natural order of things in a home— "mother" and "wife" is dominant. So when you ladies use that power well, you end up with a husband who could write this:

"The biggest surprise of marriage was that it could be a very wonderful experience and an exciting journey. I am also grateful for my spouse and neither of us ever engages in the spouse bashing that seems so prevalent in recent years among my peers. I just simply smile and think how it bites to be them. I consider myself a very lucky man with the woman I am married to . . . very blessed is a better term for it. She never nags, she is

confident in herself, and she doesn't buy into any of the 'typical' female emotional traps that us fellers cringe at—nor does she ever play emotional/mind games. So . . . don't wake me just yet . . . I wish to enjoy this dream a bit longer."

2. In what way(s) has marriage made you a better person?

- "I am a better person because of the sacrifices. I have greater patience, reliability, stability and happiness.
- "I've learned how to love with all my heart and to trust because I feel like a man, a wanted and desired being, and a complete man. I love it and how it fits."
- "I have learned to give in advance of receiving, and in some cases give without receiving. Furthermore, I can give almost without limit, given my wife's nurturing love."
- "Marriage has made me better by forcing me out of myself and living for others. In fact, I am called to do no less than lay down my life for my spouse. Some days I can say, 'Well done.' And other days I'm less than stellar. Always being called to this total giving of self saved me from total destruction."
- "I was very selfish and self-centered. She opened me up to sharing and caring about others."
- "Before marriage, my idea of a good time was going out to the bars with my friends. Now that I am married, I enjoy spending more time at home with my wife and kids than I do out at the bars. My wife has made me mature more than I ever would have imagined."
- "It has pushed me to my emotional limits and allowed me to control my emotions better!"
- "Focus on a purpose in life—taking care of family."

- "Made me responsible and kept me from doing foolish things."
- "Marriage made me a more responsible person and made me focus more clearly on obtainable goals. I could see myself as a beer-drinking, pot-smoking lout being forever twenty-one and stupid."
- "Taught me that love is not a feeling, but an action."
- "My life is more complete having a wife and kids."

Research studies have always demonstrated that men are generally medically, emotionally, physically, psychologically, and financially more well off when married. Marriage settles men down, which probably protects them from excessively risky behaviors, gives them feminine, loving caretaking, and gives them something—the family—to live for. That sense of purpose and importance is the very essence of the elixir that keeps a male yearning to be more of a man as well as making him happy.

An e-mail from Michael caps this off nicely:

"One day I was helping a friend build a fence. It was hot and he was down on his knees pouring concrete for the fence post. Our wives were both there. His wife could see that he was hot, she began to fan him with her hand and then she bent over and began to blow on his neck. I was astounded! Where do you find such a woman? Hell would freeze over before my wife would blow on my neck. My wife said that she was doing that just for effect. But I can tell you this—her husband would die for her. And all of his friends wish they could trade him places."

A well-treated husband will definitely become the best man possible.

3. What are the benefits of being married vs. single?

- "To love someone else and help serve their needs brings deeper happiness than simple hedonistic pleasure. Having someone doing the same for me gives me a trusting, happy place in the world."
- "My life is very fulfilling now. When I was single, it was filled with temporary happiness through things I could buy. This side of the coin is much better and I wish everyone could experience having such a blessing."
- "In marriage, two people can establish a virtual endless highway of giving, sharing, and love. When I was single, with each girl I dated it was like I constantly lived on a one-way street, either mine or hers. When I found my wife, all of a sudden it seemed that the road went two ways—and then things grew and developed from there into a highway of respect, love, and communication."
- "Married I always have someone on my side and someone to talk to about anything."
- "I realized a most wonderful benefit of being in a happy marriage when my wife went out of town and I came home after work to an empty house—no wife or little boy to greet me. My only thought was, 'Oh yeah, this is what it was like to be single—that bites!' I love having someone who cares and has a real interest in me to share my life with. We can talk about the trials of the day and I am able to find peace."
- "Always having someone to share your day with. Having someone there to help you through the bad times, and share the good times. Knowing that no matter what happens in life, she will always be there by your side. We can tackle life as a team—rather than alone."

- "I eat better."
- "The screaming sex drive actually can have a regular outlet with someone who loves you." "I think sex is more enjoyable because it is safer and easier to obtain." "A constant loving companion, someone who is 'in it' with you, good sex, frequent sex, good sex . . . did I say frequent sex?"
- "Raising kids."
- "You have someone to build a history with."
- "To have someone there to share with. From the **good,** to the **bad,** to the **ugly.** A partner who can help with the troubles and share in the successes; someone to laugh with, cry with, and to hug and say nothing."

The kind of call that makes me saddest is when a caller tells me a story of a husband and wife pulling apart when the bad and the ugly are pounding on their door, and their response is to turn on each other, or turn away from each other, when that is the very time they should entwine arms and defend against the bad/ugly together. I have to remind many callers of their vows concerning for better or worse, in sickness and in health, as well as not allowing anyone to turn them asunder. I often think that the vows should be on the refrigerator door and bedpost, reminding people that these issues are usually temporary if they cling to each other rather than the alternative.

Please, before you turn your back on your spouse and your marriage, consider how much you'd lose from the lists of this chapter. Perhaps this letter from Sally will help.

"For years I have been listening to your show, reading your books, and trying to walk the walk. There was a problem however in my marriage that I was having trouble facing—and as a result I was doing nothing about it. Nothing, that is, except

grieving silently inside. Then on Friday you had a caller whose problem mirrored mine. The intimacy had been lost in her marriage and she was afraid if she made the first move her husband would push her away. This is a fear that I could easily identify with. You advised her to seduce her husband and that she had to do it by the weekend.

"Okay, I said out loud to myself, 'This now applies to you too!' So, to get to the point, Dr. Laura, mission accomplished. I am writing to you with a huge smile on my face and a thank you to you for giving me the courage to physically love my wonderful man again as in my heart I always have.

"We women do have the power to make things right again. He even volunteered to fix a sink. An orgasm and a sink fixed all in one morning. Can life get any better?"

I don't think so.

Chapter 4

Dos and Don'ts

Through all the different marital mistakes that will be described in this chapter, keep three things in mind: (1) if you make changes, not *try*, but actually *make* and stay with more positive behaviors, your marriage will improve in your head (attitude is everything) and in your spouse's head, heart, and actions (unless you married a seriously disturbed individual), and (2) the difficulties, discomfort, and embarrassment involved in acknowledging your mistakes and developing new patterns of actions and reactions are worth it!

The third lesson of this chapter requires a bit more explanation. I recently received a letter from a listener who described "getting it" when my advice seems inconsistent from call to call. The example he gave was my telling a grandmother to follow the daughter-in-law's wishes about the kids' bedtime when they visit her. Another call had me telling a daughter-in-law to loosen up and let Grandma do grandparent things even when they seem to spoil the kids—that's what kids throughout the ages have enjoyed about going to Grandma's house! The listener wrote that although my advice seemed inconsistent, it wasn't if you consider my true goal: peace in the family.

To have peace, everyone's got to give a gift to the other. There is a biblical story about Aaron, the brother of Moses, dealing with two feuding neighbors who were no longer talking. Aaron met one in the public square and told him an absolute lie: "I was talking to your old friend the other day and he said nice things about you," is a reasonable paraphrase. Aaron did the same thing to the other fellow when he saw him later. Now when the two accidentally met in the square, they greeted each other warmly, in spite of the fact that their dispute was not negotiated, arbitrated, litigated, compromised, or argued out.

There are a few lessons to be gained from that story. However the most important one, and the third lesson of this chapter, is the incredible power of making the other feel cared about, special, important, valued, admired, loved, and appreciated as a real woman or a real man. That is more important than typical marital dispute resolution techniques, even compromise, making deals, and so forth; without that important sense of being adored, there will be no compromise.

Daniel, a listener, sent me a copy of a letter he gave to his wife:

"I want my wife back. I don't know who you are. You are not the person I married 27 years ago. It seems I am marginalized and relegated to the point of insignificance in your life. For you it seems there is always something more important than being my wife. This has been going on for a long time. My hope was that 'some day' things would be different.

"Your priorities have been: your mother and father, the children, work, your aunt, a friend's needs, some task that has to be finished before bed, or whatever . . . The list goes on and on. All of these are noble causes, but it leaves you with having nothing left over for me.

"I do have needs and have told you this numerous times. Your response is typically that I am some selfish, unreasonable, irrational SOB—and then anger that I keep bringing this up. You cry about it, but don't do anything to change. You just want to be angry about it and then act like you are the victim."

This is the plaintive cry of a lonely man who is losing hope. It isn't a midlife crisis that will send him into the arms of a woman who behaves excited to see him and appreciative of his company—it is too many years of emotionally devastating neglect, which is a form of spousal abuse, emotional domestic violence.

The loneliness situation in life is not actually being *alone*—it is being married to somebody to whom you appear to be invisible or have the importance of a wilted house plant. Being ignored, marginalized, disrespected, and then belittled for expressing your pain is a level of pain that is unbearable.

One of the biggest mistakes spouses make is not making much of an effort at all. If it isn't fun or easy then it isn't worth doing? Obligations and responsibilities don't require "feeling like it," they require honor and compassion. Whether it is sex and affection, showing interest in the activities and passions of your spouse, giving up something important to you because it would make family peace and/or a happy spouse, you are required by your vows to function out of commitment, rather than running on *your* immediate needs or feelings.

I know it is no longer a popular notion to give when "ya' don't feel like it," but this is the best route to a wonderful closeness and the most intimate feelings that are unimaginable if you focus in on only what suits you.

What follows is a list of dos and don'ts to help you avoid and/or repair some of the common mistakes in marriage.

TAKING EACH OTHER FOR GRANTED

"Guys take good wives for granted and don't see them as the crown jewel of their lives," wrote another listener, John. T.J., a listener, admits that *"Men take a lot for granted, especially if our wives are good cooks, good mothers, etc. These characteristics aren't 'sexy' when compared to a pretty single woman that you could be with, but they are so important."*

When a husband treats his wife's attention to the home, meals, laundry, child care, and so forth with quiet acceptance, he begins to relegate her to being his mother instead of his woman. I have told many a husband who has called my radio program to frequently express gratitude to his wife for "making the home a beautiful garden with the sights and smells of heaven." Sounds corny? Then use your own words!

Don't think that you are *entitled* to all the responsibilities and loving actions of your spouse; **Do** behave as though every mundane gesture of your beloved is a direct *gift* from heaven.

Don't think you don't need to make pleasing your beloved a priority because he/she is already yours; **Do** think that every day is an opportunity to forge a stronger bond between you.

Don't assume that all or even most of the problems of the marriage are his/hers; **Do** come up with changes you *know* you need to make to be a better husband/wife . . . and do them!

Don't wait for your spouse to make changes before you make the ones you know you should make; **Do** make an offering of your part even though you feel hurt, angry, or embarrassed, because that change in your actions/attitude will likely have two wonderful effects: (1) you will discover that you can create more of your own happiness with your own change in behavior and attitude and (2) your spouse will be motivated by your actions . . . and around it goes!

Mindy discovered the power of this last **Don't/Do,** when after complaining repetitively and bitterly to her husband about being unhappy with the role of an at-home mom, wife, and homemaker.

> *"For some reason I wasn't happy. I spent weeks telling him how bad our marriage was and that if we didn't get help soon, we would fall apart. After many fights about how he did not ever do the little things for me, and how much more I needed from him, he told me that I would not get anything until I started to keep up my end of the deal. I protested that this is a marriage and not a deal. He agreed, then told me to do my part of the marriage.*
>
> *"I decided that I would 'do my part' for a few weeks—and do it better than ever. After a few weeks, I would then bring up the issue and finish it! I would prove that I deserved more. After only one week of doing my part everything changed. He was doing more than I had ever asked him to do. All of the little things were being taken care of as well as the big ones—and some I didn't even know about.*
>
> *"I had started treating him as though he was number one on my list. As soon as I did that he helped me to realize that I have always been number one on his list—but I was just too busy (complaining and pouting). I forgot my role. I am truly sorry for doing this to my husband. He is the best man I have ever known. He loves me with all of his heart, and I will spend the rest of my life trying to love him better."*

Love Alert! To paraphrase an e-mail from a repentant spouse: treat your spouse like the catch they are, do not let careers and hobbies get in the way of time together, don't let debt and possessions possess you and bring turmoil and blame, don't use your spouse when you need what you need and then ignore them and their needs, leaving them to fend for themselves until you get lonely and need something for yourself again; don't be haughty and lazy about the priority of love in marriage and your responsibility to make them feel loved and important to you and the family.

Your Tip: Write a letter to your husband/wife today, telling them specific and general things they do/are that are spectacular; cover everything from their sacrifices, activities, manliness/femininity, successes, character, being great role models for your children, sexiness and sensuality, compassion, and so forth. For example: "Thank you for showing our sons how to use a drill, chop firewood, change a tire, do income taxes, and all the other things that tend to fall under 'Dad's Duties,' " or "Thank you for homeschooling our children so they can be guided and educated to their full potential."

As you write your letter, you will find immediately that you will begin to feel happier in your marriage simply by focusing in on the good and the great instead of how your attention is generally drawn toward the negative and annoying trivialities. The second thing that will happen is that you will ignite a loving reaction from your spouse that will keep your marriage warm for a long time.

"ME" VERSUS "WE"

A good start to not taking a marital partner for granted is to think in *we* terms more often than *me* terms. Don't take this to the extreme, of course. It is good and even necessary for each of you to have some different interests, hobbies, friends, buddy time, free time, and so forth; your individuality needs to be nurtured and respected. Now here's the big HOWEVER: it is a bad mistake to selfishly guard your right to do and be what you want without respect for your duties as a spouse.

I had a woman caller recently whose husband was not coming to their three-and-a-half-year-old son's rodeo appearance where the kids, led by a parent, all dressed up cowboy/girl style and paraded around the arena. My caller wondered what she could do about this.

> **DrL:** Well, the first obvious question is why won't he be there?
>
> **Valerie:** He says he'll have folks there with whom he does business and one shouldn't mix business and pleasure.
>
> **DrL (long hesitation):** That's not the truth. I don't know what the truth is, but that ain't it. You know your man—I don't—why would he not show up? (Repetitive nagging on my part ensued.)
>
> **Valerie:** I don't know.
>
> **DrL:** Come on, Valerie, tell me, is he typically neglectful or self-centered?
>
> **Valerie:** Yes. That's been an ongoing problem.
>
> **DrL:** So you know the real reason then?
>
> **Valerie:** Yeah, I think he wanted that time to practice for himself and didn't want to give it up for our son.
>
> **DrL:** My dear, you've got to sit him down tonight and get him refocused on what makes him a man in your eyes.
>
> **Valerie:** Okay.

I got an e-mail the very next day from Valerie, happily letting me know that her husband had heard our call and had
gone to his son's event and had taken tons of pictures.

*"I'm pretty sure my phone call to you was the straw that broke
the camel's back. He knew he was in the wrong which is why
we couldn't get him on the air with you but he really struggled
with postponing his time with his horses. Plus he really values
your show and I have seen such a difference in our relationship since he has started listening to you. But he still resorts to
his old 'selfish' habits from time to time—but I'm right there,
gently nudging him in the right direction! And, our son won
third place in his first little junior rodeo—and I could tell my
husband was proud!"*

"Gently nudging," as opposed to screaming, ranting, and
threatening, is what helps a spouse grow in the "us/we"
department. Selfishness is generally a lifelong characteristic
and requires gentle nudging before—and enthusiastic kudos
after—to help someone grow into being joyous about giving
without feeling as though they are giving up something more
important . . . themselves.

Basically it comes down to this: if you don't think about
we/us (spouse and children) you will lose track of each other,
feel disconnected and alone. The simple act of a wedding ceremony or childbirth does not ensure ongoing bliss and bonding—that's where the work comes in. I'm sorry to even use
the word "work," because it is often used synonymously with
burden; well, maybe sometimes our obligations do feel like
burdens, and when that's so, we call forging ahead honoring
one's commitment. When each of you makes those efforts to
honor the commitment, you will each have more respect and
deeper love and sense of loyalty to one another.

Chasing career and personal goals with little regard to the impact it is having on your spouse and family is a map where all roads dead-end. Men who do this usually end up with heart attacks; women who do this end up with out-of-control families (as the parenting and home atmosphere are sidelined) and Valium drips.

I'm convinced that *most* affairs are due to two things: a spouse feeling ignored or a spouse feeling overwhelmed. In both those situations, flirting and sexual affairs are considered "medicinal." When these affairs are followed up with divorces, children's lives are destroyed, and the remaining husband/wife is left with defensive anger, confusion, regret, and profound loss.

Don't think first about what you're getting or losing at any one moment; **Do** think about how putting your spouse before yourself makes your spouse feel cherished.

Don't insist on your opinion or way of looking at things as the only way; **Do** check with your spouse about his/her way of handling a particular issue to see if there might be a solution that incorporates the wisdom you both have, as in "two heads are better than one."

Don't focus so much on making sure "my needs are met"; **Do** prioritize the needs of the union—you are now "us/we," and not primarily "me."

It is important that spouses pay attention to staying connected. Have date nights, to flirt and chatter—so you can remember why you married in the first place.

Love Alert! "It's my way or the highway," works when you are the boss, but it is not a sentiment that endears lovers to each other. Never assume that your way of thinking and doing things is the only possible way. Don't assume that your spouse will automatically have or absorb your attitudes about sex, communication, housework, lawn mowing, budgeting and spending, and so forth. Instead of feeling threatened by difference or possible change, look at it as a way of expanding your universe.

When there is a difference in opinion or desire, a good rule is to allow the person with the most invested or the most passion about that issue to make the decision. Two things come from that: (1) you make them happy and when they're happy, they're more likely to be motivated to make you happy, and (2) when people are given power, rather than having to arm wrestle for it, they tend to use that power more benevolently. Over the span of sixty or so great marital years together, it will go back and forth many times; don't get stuck on one moment in six decades!

IT WAS OKAY, NOW IT'S NOT OKAY

"When listening to you talk to some men and women, I hear them complain how bad their marriages are and how difficult their spouses are. I also know that every marriage reaches a time that I call 'The Honeymoon is Over Time (THIOT).' As much as the beloved was idealized early on—their faults are seen with as much intensity," writes Dorothy.

THIOT is a universal phenomenon. Why? Because when people yearn to bond and be loved and secure within a relationship they are highly motivated, of course, to succeed. That means that when gargoyles present themselves, that is imperfect habits, behavior patterns, preferences and interests, the beholder of these gargoyles, wanting a "happy ending" (marriage), will ignore them, rationalize them, deny being negatively impacted, manipulate to make them (temporarily) disappear, or have the fantasy that it'll all magically work out and get better if we just keep talking and talking and talking about it or just get married.

Valerie called about this very issue. She is twenty-seven, married four years to a man in whom she imagined great potential. He recently went on a trip to visit his folks, and when he came back he announced he was going to quit his umpteenth job/career and wanted to postpone having children for at least a decade. He also expressed how tired he was feeling like a lump of clay for her to punch, pinch, and mold, and wanted her to be satisfied with him as he was—albeit not mature, stable, or responsible as yet. This was a boy.

Valerie, being a decent and kindly young woman, felt compassion for the pain he was expressing; that impressed me about her. Valerie was also devastated—her gamble did not pay off. I urged her to live in the land of "what is," and permanently vacate her condo in the land of "wish it were."

Most of the time, however, the situation is not this entirely out of focus. Most of these disappointments with reality are smaller, like, for instance, Mike's case.

> *"Being absentminded is my problem. When we were dating, it happened as well, and for a time, she thought it was cute. I clearly remember telling her at the time that absentmindedness was a big fault of mine and that after we were married she wouldn't think it to be cute or funny at all. Boy, was I right!*
>
> *"Anyway, I have to write things down all the time as I am living proof of Mark Twain's theory that mental notes are not worth the paper they're written on."*

Women do have more of a tendency to label annoying behaviors and characteristics as cute or funny before marriage.

Men have more of a tendency to simply ignore them. Mark admits that his wife's dislike of anything to do with sports is annoying. He knew about this mismatch issue when they were dating. *"During our dating, I should have focused less on the sexual and more on how we fit together in the other ways. I see no solution for this. I've tried many times and in different ways to even understand it. We share many things together and I would like nothing more than to share these awesome recreational experiences with her."*

What is the saving grace in Mark's situation? It is that he has to embrace and celebrate the other "many things together," and realize that those "awesome recreational experiences" can be with buddies; with his woman, he has the rest of his being to share.

I typically beseech people calling my show ready to marry someone of another religion to rethink that decision. Usually, the scenario takes one of three forms: (1) "Religion doesn't matter to me, anyway," or (2) "We'll just have a two-religion family and bring the children up knowing both," or (3) "He/she is going to let me raise the children my way in my church."

Big mistakes. Generally as one gets older and children enter the equation, one's religion (roots) gets more important. The dissension between spouses who wish to pull the other one their way is often very destructive to the marriage and family functioning. The two-religion concept doesn't work because neither spouse has someone to share with and the children end up painting matzo for Easter; the family is fragmented in a most meaningful arena. *"My mistake is that I did not marry a girl who shared my religion. My wife converted when we married, but within a few years decided it was not for her and has not practiced since. I have missed out on sharing my religion with someone I care about. This mistake is not fixable because her religion is her choice, not mine,"* explained Daniel, a listener.

It is not unusual for people to underestimate the importance of *common* values, goals, and ideals because they're swept away by sexual pleasures; this has been a strong argument against unmarried sex which virtually eradicates rational, objective thinking and assessment. When people have great, exciting sex and a lot of fun together, they often imagine marriage a simple extension of those pleasures throughout all eternity.

When there is a basis of trust, honor, and devotion, people can weather the storms of incompatibility in matters of lesser importance, but on the big ones *"there remains a wall that prevents true intimacy, which on my part at least, is a constant source of loneliness and frustration,"* admits Tom, another listener.

Some things cannot be fixed; they must be endured. When some things cannot be endured, honorably and positively, they usually have to be terminated. It is amazing, though, how many people of past generations have chosen "to endure" and, over time, when they've treated each other not with disdain, but with respect, have come to embrace more issues together.

I have always found that the key to frustration with one's spouse is the difference between *expectation* and *reality*. Other than psychosis or coma, I know no way to escape reality! This then leaves expectation as the adjustable quality. If you expect your spouse to change, and you are frustrated because they don't, try dropping the expectation altogether, or changing it to the opposite. If your spouse, for example, tends to be messy, expect the messy and don't fight about it anymore. If a lack of clutter is important to you, more important than it is to them, neaten it up yourself! If you expect them to be sloppy and they do something to neaten up, well, won't that be a delightful hoot! Be sure to tell 'em how much you appreciated the thought!

Many a time when you're frustrated by their annoying

trait, there might just be a logical explanation for things gone wrong. Please don't jump immediately to assuming they set out to hurt you. One absolute necessity in any marriage is the inherent belief that the other has your best interest at heart. So, please, always leave room for benefit of the doubt!

Don't imagine you're going to change your spouse by complaining, hating, punishing, demeaning, threatening, or manipulating; **Do** know that you can change your view of your spouse and your marriage by finding something each day about your spouse that brings you pleasure, pride, or gratitude.

Don't choose to dwell on the annoying qualities of your spouse; **Do** remind yourself each time you're annoyed with him/her of at least three qualities you admire and enjoy.

Don't believe for a moment that you aren't annoying too!; **Do** acknowledge to yourself and to him/her that you both brought a lot of baggage into the marriage to unpack and that you promise to be more aware and considerate of your impact on him/her.

Love Alert! "*I think that husbands and wives forget why they picked one another. They think there is something magic that happens when they marry that erases the irritating things and automatically brings people closer . . . the reality is that marriage is a magnifying glass for irritations, but it also helps if you remember what drew you to one another in the first place. I think also that gratitude is way underused in marriages,*" explained Kris. Kris went on to say that marriage is a daily dose of humble pie. Her husband is patient, calm, and good-spirited, while she describes herself as volatile, reactionary, and somewhat snooty. "*My husband is a daily reminder of the joy that comes from living with grace, and I try to take that lesson in each and every day."*

Kris is an example of an essential aspect of marriage; instead of glomming onto the bad, which admittedly can be annoying stuff, use each day to learn something about yourself from your spouse's role-modeling of quality characteristics.

PRIVACY BETRAYAL

Part A: Let's imagine for a moment that you did something reasonably stupid, bad, self-centered, thoughtless . . . you get the idea . . . to your spouse. Part B: You then have remorse, take responsibility, attempt to repair the problem, and make efforts to never repeat it. You think that "it's over," until you realize that his/her parents and family and most of your common friends know all about it. How do you feel? Humiliated? Betrayed?

This is a common mistake that married folks make because they either want folks to side with them, so they can feel superior to their spouse or more justified in their rage of victimhood, or they want the attention that complaining and public suffering brings.

When we truly want help with a problem, we don't present it to friends and relatives as, "Woe is me—look what he/she did to ME!" When we truly want help we humbly go to clergy, counselor, close friend, or trusted family member who will focus in on *ourselves;* how we may be distorting things, how we may be overreacting, how we may have contributed to the problem, how our perception might be off, and so forth.

"The biggest mistake I see my friends make," writes Pete, *"is*

telling their friends about their problems instead of going to each other within the marriage. It only builds resentment and if the information is leaked—which it usually is—then the trust is gone, making the problem even worse."

Meredith offered that whenever she feels annoyed, *"I remind myself that I'm sure I'm at least twice as annoying as whatever he is doing. I also NEVER EVER discuss 'issues' with anyone. If it's important enough for me to want to tell other people, that's my signal I should consider discussing the topic with my husband—or just let it go. But NEVER go outside the marriage to discuss disagreements."*

Another form of "going outside the marriage" when there are problems is becoming available to listen to someone else's problems. When a husband or wife starts tending to the emotions of someone else, kidding themselves that this is all about friendly compassion, it is the beginning of an emotional affair—which could lead to adultery. Putting yourself in the position of being special to a member of the opposite sex is another form of "medicine" for what's ailing you: your relationship. It's funny, in a sad way, that folks will choose to be more compassionate, listening supportively to a stranger, when they resentfully withhold this behavior from the so-called "love of their lives."

Spending an inordinate amount of time with your buddies, friends, or mommy is another form of rejection of your spouse. Granted, some of you might find more peace outside your own homes, but abdicating and gravitating away from home will not offer much in the way of repair or growth.

The straw that broke the camel's back in my listener Margaret's first marriage ("in my twenties, no children—except maybe 'us.'") was when she suggested to her husband that they repaint the apartment together and hang new curtains. This was her attempt to have them work together on their nest as a positive move in a troubled situation. He told her that he'd have to ask his mother. Camel died right there. Letting family influence decisions whether big or small in your marriage is to be a child playing grown-up.

Don't use discussions about how bad your spouse is as entertainment with your friends; **Do** take every opportunity you can to build up your spouse in your mind by relating wonderful, positive stories.

Don't escape from contentious issues with your spouse by avoiding home and hanging with family or friends or at the local bar . . . and don't even think of an affair; **Do** walk into your home with something generous to say and kind to do and watch the immediate change in your home environment.

Don't let your family or friends determine or influence what happens in your home and marital relationship—do not take polls with them to decide anything about your home life; **Do** have the courage of your own opinions and the respect for those of your beloved to make your own joint decisions.

Love Alert! *"Husbands and wives forget to maintain the boundaries of their marriage and this causes so many problems. My husband and I do not share our arguments with others; we do not speak poorly of each other, we don't call each other names or swear at each other; we are always loyal to each other first. I don't keep things from my husband or tell my girlfriends secrets that my husband doesn't know. We don't allow other people to interfere in our marriage. If we have a problem that we can't handle, we have agreed that we will go seek the advice of a professional,"* commented Jacquilyne.

TALKING ABOUT ... WHATEVER

Women often complain that their husbands never talk about their feelings and the relationship, and that they won't listen without giving advice. Men often complain that their wives talk incessantly about their feelings, are defensive when they try to give their opinion, and repeat themselves over and over and don't seem to want to actually do anything about the problem—just talk about it.

Both are correct. There are inherent difficulties in communication between men and women; most difficulties are surmountable—as long as each is willing to understand, accept, and somewhat cater to the characteristics of masculinity and femininity.

Paul, a listener, wrote that a typical woman mistake in a marriage is to believe that the husband's silence is solid evidence that he is happy and satisfied in the marriage.

> *"Far from it. I wholeheartedly agree with Dr. Laura when she explains to women callers on her radio show that men are not their girl friends. Men are stoic, and women are gabby. Men survive by enduring, while women must have been born to converse.*
>
> *"If a woman expects her husband to express his dissatisfaction with some part of a marriage, she is sorely mistaken. I believe a man would rather walk naked on hot burning coals than express a concern about his marriage to his wife. He doesn't have the skills to converse at her level, and why complain when he is likely to generate only denial, anger, tears, or (worst of all) denial of sex?*
>
> *"So we endure silently . . ."*

Even assuming that a man and woman love and care for one another, a lack of a sense of freedom to express oneself to one's beloved without fireworks or punishment is profoundly deadly to a relationship. *"If one hesitates to speak for fear of the other's reaction, that person will close down and not only will the couple not solve whatever problem they have, but resentment will build. Few things hurt worse than the thought that your loved one does not care about your concerns. Even if an answer does not readily present itself, just the thought that your spouse cares enough to listen, and not immediately get defensive or judge, can make all the difference,"* explained Randy, a male listener.

Lori, another listener, wrote that she believes the best thing she and her husband did for their relationship while dating was to agree to be brutally honest with each other. Neither has to wonder or guess what is going on with the other, nor do they get confronted two years after the fact with ancient hurts that they cannot remember, much less defend. Once a problem is addressed and it is over, she explained, it *is* over. This makes for a relationship with a lot of security *if* each is mature, emotionally healthy, and generous enough to be willing and able to sustain themselves through the uncomfortable and unpleasant part of working something out.

Bradley admitted to having trouble with communication because he takes it all so personally: *"It's hard for me to listen to her problems, issues, or whatever, and just listen. I feel like because she is with me that she has issues or problems, and I take it personally— like I am not a good enough husband. I think I am overly sensitive sometimes and I get frustrated, which is only counterproductive."*

I get a large number of calls from people who wonder why their spouses haven't told them things. Generally, as evolves during the call, it is because the spouse is afraid of the repercussions—and by repercussions I don't mean appropriate consequences for inappropriate activities. The repercussions mostly have to do with the communication being filtered through one's own insecurities, assumptions, and perceptions, without truly hearing the message of the other person.

What is the solution to this hypersensitivity? Manual override. That means you work very hard to keep your fears out of the way of your ears. If your beloved is telling you that someone came on to them at work or the grocery store, your first reaction *should* be to be pleased that they are open with you about what happened. People having affairs or flirting their brains out usually don't share this information, do they? Besides, as I often have to remind callers/listeners, no one can yank a happy spouse from your arms, so keep your spouse feeling loved and valued; this is more powerful than screaming paranoid nasty comments!

When your spouse has done something stupid or wrong with finances, home electronics, the car—whatever—the one person in the universe they should be able to come to is you. And when they do come to you first, be there for them. If the two of you can't talk about everything without one of you behaving like a ferocious parent, how can you expect them to ever come to you again or feel safe with you and loving toward you?

It is sadly typical for spouses to say, "I want you to be able to come to me and talk about anything," but when the spouse takes you up on it you break down, get hysterical and punitive, and then manipulate the situation so that you're the poor victim and they have to take back everything they tried to work out with you.

One woman, for example, called my show to complain to me that her husband complained to her that he's tired of her gaining weight and not taking care of her appearance or health. My question to her was, "Well, is it true? Are you fat and sloppy or not? If you are, why can't he express dismay over something that *is* under your control and is an obligation of yours?" She had been trying to turn it around to make him insensitive and hurtful for simply expressing his unhappiness that "his woman" wasn't doing her best to stay his woman.

For women it is usually weight, sex, and her intrusive family that they don't want to converse about; for men it is more typically their overworking, drinking, and finances. Where there are taboo areas because of sensitivity, where no conversation is permitted without defensive hostility, recrimination, and payback, those areas become the assassins of intimacy and love.

Merritt, a listener, had this general advice concerning bad things to avoid in communicating: "*Don't expect your spouse to read your mind and then get bent out of shape when it doesn't happen. Saying one thing, meaning another, and then punishing your spouse when words are taken at face value is another no-no. Pick your battles carefully. Never name-call and don't dredge up old, dead, and should-be-buried stuff to throw in a spouse's face.*"

Some people communicate only to win, dominate, and protect their own self-image and ego. To that end, they attack viciously and say things that cannot ever be taken back. Watch your words, for if you leave deep enough wounds, your beloved will not ever be able to share his/her heart with you again. Some things are too terrible to be forgiven or forgotten.

Nobody really enjoys hearing that their spouse is dissatisfied with something about them or the relationship; fears of judgment and rejection rise up. However if you stuff your childlike insecurities, and rise to the occasion of hearing whatever it is he/she has to say to you, you actually increase their respect for you as well as have the opportunity to make life better for them. This is how you build that feeling in them of cherishing you and grateful that they chose you in the first place.

Jenny learned that lesson mainly because her husband was so understanding:

"I learned to bottle up all my feelings and to never speak about anything that was bothering me because my mother raised me to believe that my problems had no merit because hers were always worse. Until I was married I didn't even realize I had this defensive behavior. Then when I had concerns with my husband, I would hold it all in until some random event would push me over the edge and I would cry and whine about things that were months past.

"Luckily I married a wonderful man, and he always asked me why I hadn't told him anything earlier, and asked why I was afraid to talk to him. I was afraid he would become angry because that was the reaction my mother always gave me.

"I had to find the strength within myself to break through the barrier I had created within myself and force myself to communicate. It's been amazing and has had such a wonderful impact on my marriage."

Sometimes you'll need to curb your anger and help each other along.

Timing is also important. Calling each other at work or in the middle of child care to express hurt, anger, upset or concern about some issue, may not be the best choice if you want your spouse's calm attention. A more typical mistake in the timing issue is dumping on each other the minute you come back together at the end of the day. I usually suggest people hug, kiss, flirt, play with the kids, and have dinner before they get into the unpleasant stuff.

What is supremely difficult is to be kind and respectful when you're mad or hurt. In this regard, please remember, marriage is not about unconditional love. You can definitely cause your spouse to love you less if you're continuously hurtful, disrespectful, and generally not cautious about their feelings. Make sure you're thinking about longevity in the marriage before you open your mouth.

Before I go on with more communication tips, let me reinforce a key concept: **communication is not just about complaints!** If more than 20 percent of your "communications" are about problems, even neutral ones like about the dishwasher, you are cruising for a bruising. Most of your communications should be about telling your spouse how happy he/she makes you, cute things the kids did, compliments, and so forth. Forgetting to keep love fresh is the worst communication mistake of all.

If you are aware that the two of you bicker constantly, the fastest way to stop this is for you, unilaterally, to stop. When folks call me complaining that their marriage is one long argument, I ask them immediately why *they* choose to argue or fight. An argument takes two; you can decide to be calm, nondefensive, reasonable, understanding, and compassionate without ever discussing new styles of communication with your spouse! You alone can change the destiny of your marriage.

Dedicate yourself to not getting sucked into the fray. You will find that no matter the subject, no matter how high the emotions, you will be able to help create a better environment for working out problems. When your spouse is no longer confronted with another angry spouse, he/she will tone down and you will be amazed at how dramatically different your relationship will become.

Don't speak out of anger; **Do** remind yourself that you love him/her just before you express yourself.

Don't make your spouse have to keep secrets from you; **Do** become the safest place to discuss everything and anything by listening without dismissing or attacking.

Don't think that all communication is with words; **Do** realize, accept, and enjoy that there are little things you're both doing for each other that say, "I love you," just as loudly.

In Summary:

For You Men: You have probably spent too much energy trying to solve all your wife's problems or complaints, only to find out she isn't bringing you a problem to fix, she just wanted to vent. Perhaps you might ask her, "Darling face, before you go on, do you want me to be the 'problem-solving husband' or the "just be quiet and listen husband'?"

Glenn, another listener, has another solution for the reality that women love to talk about "tragedies" and "issues" not only once, but again and again. He and his wife have instituted The Ten Minute Rule.

> *"When my woman comes home from work, she has ten minutes to unload the day's tragedies. Whatever the tragedy, I will sit and listen. It's her time and she needs to use it wisely. When the long pause comes, I simply ask, 'What's my role? Are you asking for a solution or am I just listening?' Most of the time I'm just listening.*
>
> *"The whole theory behind The Ten Minute Rule is that women have a man that listens to what's serious to her. The rest of the night is left to live life: biking, hiking, golf, sex, movies, dinner, planning a trip, playing with the kids, watching the sunset—all the things that make the memories of a good life."*

For You Women: Please remember that if you want to just talk and talk about something, turn to your girl friends, sisters, and mother before you imagine that your husband will make a good girl friend. Men fix things; it is in their nature. Men are not insensitive or inconsiderate by birth—they are just geared for action. As I tell my women callers, explain yourself to your man in such a way as to give him an assignment—they're great at that!

Also remember if you communicate with your man as a mother would talk to an errant teenager, you're probably not going to get the best results. Approach your man as though you see him as such and you will get great results. Men do best with crystal clear clarity as to what you mean and want—they're not terrific at interpreting what you mean so mean what you say.

SEX

Good marital sex is when both are sensitive to the needs of the other. Sex is a very important part of a marriage because it creates a physical and emotional bond. As David, a listener, added: *"Sex is like oil to an engine. It can be the thing that helps to cool the friction and stress that will naturally arise."*

Dan commented: *"Good marital sex is all about giving . . . giving your partner what they want and desire. An unwillingness to give indicates a selfishness that will ruin things both in and out of the marital bed. The gifts that couples give to one another in the marital sexual relationship have to be among the most cherished gifts of all. You open yourself completely to your spouse; you are completely vulnerable. It is a time when you trust the most. It is that giving of oneself and the receiving by their spouse that makes the sex so great."*

Yet with all this tender, spiritual, and loving sensitivity about the meaning of passionate marital sexuality, the typical letter or call I get from a husband sounds like the following letter from Dallas:

> *"My wife informed me earlier this year that she just doesn't have any interest in sex anymore (she is 36 and I am 40). I can't remember a time of intimacy in the last 5 years that she didn't make me feel that she was 'allowing' me to have 'make it quick' sex with her, and without making me feel pathetic about the urge. Her refusal to do anything at all that she doesn't 'feel like' doing has robbed me of all the joy in my life, both in my marriage and motivation for work. It is affecting my children in that they don't get the chance to see love and affection between their parents.*
>
> *"What an amazing blessing it must be for men who have wives that actually contemplate their husband's feelings and happiness and think about doing the simple things that make a man feel like a man.*
>
> *"I am drudging through a day at a time, hoping that when my daughters are grown and out, that I will still have the energy and desire to go out and find someone who I might share my joy, achievements, and affection. That's the only hope for a man who will never spend a single day away from my girls as they grow, and who has a wife that says, 'get over it, you're married . . . go take care of yourself in the shower.' "*

Frankly I have been amazed at how blatant and cruel so many wives have become over the issue of their marital intimacy. Women call me to complain about their husband's desire for them all the time. Complain! As if being desired were some kind of intrusion or insult. These women excuse themselves from intimacy with their husbands because:

- I was molested and I'm turned off to sex.

- I don't like my body.

- I'm busy and tired with work, school, kids, relatives, and household things.

- I have too much on my mind.

- It's disgusting that all he wants is sex, sex, sex.

- He should just accept and understand I'm just not interested.

- I just don't feel like it.

- I'm bored sexually.

Get over yourselves and get under your men (although most men enjoy their women on top too)! If you don't, when the kids are up and out, he'll likely go with them.

These would likely also be the first wives to complain that their husbands don't do enough around the house, that they have virtual sex while looking at pictures of naked women online, and can't seem to remember Valentine's Day. No kidding.

Sex for men is like talking is for women with respect to feeling loved, cared about, and special.

Nancy, a listener, wrote that she always wondered and questioned why God blessed men with a greater sex drive than women.

"I felt my husband's needs were really unnecessary and that he merely just needed to curb his appetite.

"Fortunately I did marry a man and not a 'guy' and he patiently put up with me in this area of our marriage for 30 years. However, after listening to your show and your detailed explanations of man's needs vs. woman's, and that men really do need the intimacy and all that goes along with it, just this simple attitude change has made all the difference for me and opened up a whole new world of intimacy between me and my sweet, dear husband."

I am often challenged by an angry woman with the question "Am I obligated to have sex with my husband? Even when I don't feel like it?" My answer has always been the same. "Yes, the same way he is obligated to go to work and support the family even when he doesn't feel like it." Sexuality is a very important part of the covenant of marriage.

My next answers are: "Do you remember ever having an orgasm? Wasn't it fun? Didn't it feel good? Doesn't a great orgasm just melt all the cares and troubles of the day away? Don't you feel happier you're married, and to him? Don't you love the feeling of being a sensual woman? Don't you sleep better afterward? Why would you want to give that up?"

Most women have to get it into their heads that enjoying their own sexuality and sensuality is not slave labor to a husband, but a beautiful, meaningful way to lead their own lives.

Even the most resistant women discover that when they "do it anyway," they do get turned on and have a great time.

And that's where you guys come in: you have to know how to "light her fire," with sensual talk, gestures, and pleasures. In other words, make sure she gets the payoff!

Julie discovered, after listening to me explaining all of this again and again on my radio program, that being sexual with her husband has led to her appreciating him more and more each day. Without this element, people become crass roommates.

"Our sex life has become a wonderful way of building our bond, relieving the day-to-day stress, and just having a good ol' time. Today I discovered one more of the many side benefits from actually ENJOYING my husband and our sex life. He's so mellow and forgiving of my (occasional) stupidity. I wrecked a pipe on our property. Once I made the call to get the cost of fixing it, I owned up to it today to my husband. His response? We are going to have some hot and heavy 'bonding' tonight so that I can make it up to him. What a deal! Life is good and my husband is wonderful."

And for you women who think marital sex is repetitive and boring . . . it is all in your attitude:

"I have never watched Desperate Housewives; *however, I have heard about it. I must admit I am one. I am a married woman who sleeps with a married man who is a devoted husband and loved Dad. I also have sex with our landscape maintenance man, the plumber, and the electrician. I wear my purple satin baby-doll pajamas for a former Marine and a computer geek who fixes what I mess up on our home system. If we had a pool, I am sure I would sleep with the pool guy too.*

"The teenager I sleep with is a real cutie! Well, he is not really a teenager but he sometimes acts like one and it is a real

turn-on! Oh, don't let me forget that I sleep with my golf and bowling buddy too.

"Just eighteen months into my marriage I slept with the chauffeur who taxied me to the hospital and held my hand before and after my radical mastectomy. This chauffeur also accompanied me to, and sat with me through all of my chemotherapy. Afterward, he would massage my back while I was throwing up and cursing the world. That same chauffeur tells me I am his 'Babe-a-licious' when we shower together.

"I guess I must be a desperate housewife because I am desperately in love with my husband who has played all of these roles throughout our marriage. He is always full of surprises and every day I ask myself, 'Who will be my next lover?' "

You cannot tell me this letter from Penny doesn't grab you where you live.

The husbands who refuse sexual intimacy are generally exceptions: ones married but homosexual, severely emotionally damaged and unable to be intimate with their woman as they don't perceive of themselves as men, have medical issues that interfere with performance, serious depression, addictions, feeling emasculated by wife, and so forth.

Don't ever (unless desperately ill) reject an amorous approach by your beloved; **Do** make your beloved feel such by some degree of physicality combined with words of love and praise.

Don't complain that your beloved is a lousy lover and not making you "happy"; **Do** compliment them when they're "getting warmer" (it is so motivating) and actually show them what would turn on your ignition switch.

Don't let your day or your history rob you of your right to marital ecstasy; **Do** make at least as much time for your "love" life with your spouse as you do for all the other stuff you consider important.

Love Alert! There is plenty of easily available information about sex. One woman listener gave this list of "suggestions" for a good and smart wife to follow:

1. Go to your local sexual products store: lubricants, toys, etc. Purchase some. Take them home and use them.
2. Remember that men are visual creatures. Purchase some naughty lingerie. Take it home and wear it for your husband. Don't worry about it being uncomfortable—it won't be on long.
3. Go to a salon and get a Brazilian wax. It will hurt something fierce, but he will really appreciate the effort. Keep yourself groomed down there—that shows you have an interest in sex. Oh, and keep your legs shaved.
4. Send the kids to Grandma's. Make love on the couch and kitchen table.
5. Go get a book on the Kama Sutra . . . they publish them with drawings and they have them nonpornographic. There are about five hundred different positions. Try them all, then you won't get bored with the same old thing.
6. Say YES more than NO. Be generous and affectionate. Read *The Proper Care and Feeding of Husbands*—understand it and put it in practice.
7. Call your husband at work. Verify you are not on the speaker phone and proceed to tell him just what you will do to him when he gets

home . . . or what you want him to do for you.
Leave naughty notes in his briefcase.

Yes, this takes effort—but it is effort that will make
both your lives more worth living . . . together!

MARITAL SIBLING RIVALRY

I was still recovering from feminism when we had Deryk. I
told my husband, not discussed—told!—that he'd better be
doing 50 percent of everything from diapers to hands-on time
with the baby. I wanted to make sure I wasn't used and abused
because I was the woman. Horrifying, actually, to remember
thinking in this bizarre way. Anyway, once Deryk was here,
I would sneak to change his diapers over 90 percent of the
time! Why? Because it was so much darn fun! He would laugh
through the whole adventure and I so loved that joyous, happy,
and loving bonding time. Having Deryk cured me finally from
feminism. I learned that domesticity was not a put-down at all;
it was the power to set the tone for the whole family experience, starting with the ambiance of the home. Houses become
homes when women make them so.

As Scott, one of my listeners, wrote: "*The biggest mistake
in a marriage is looking too much at the 'weight and balance' scale
of who is doing what for whom and measuring responses accordingly.
Giving your all, acting correctly regardless of circumstance, should be
the goal.*"

One of the best descriptions and explanations of this
destructive "keeping score" mentality came from a listener. To
paraphrase: Both sexes make this mistake. And what makes the

score-keeping double trouble is that men and women score things differently.

For a woman, her man going to work and bringing home a paycheck gets one point. To her, laundry, floors, child care, shopping, cooking, and maybe even sex? is one point every time she does it. So when she measures her day against his, she has accumulated fifty points (probably minus the sex point . . . 'cause she's mad) and he only has one. That means when he comes through the door she jumps on him to "pull his weight" at home, and that leads to resentment on both sides.

From a man's point of view, his going through traffic to work, dealing with bosses and coworkers and clients, meetings, paperwork, stress, and so forth is worth thousands of points. Compared to his bringing home the "bread," he sees what she's doing as comfortable, convenient, arbitrary, and relatively simple—so he gives it all maybe five points. After having done that math, he doesn't understand why she gets angry because he doesn't want to do anything when he comes in the door.

Our culture has made two things perfectly clear: anything she does that benefits her husband points out her oppression; if he doesn't do at least half her work once he comes home from his work, he's a heartless, lazy, selfish bastard who doesn't care about her or the family.

Karen describes rescuing herself from this typical and destructive mind-set:

> *"I'm married to a wonderful man, and our marriage is as close to perfect as I could dream of . . . but in the beginning I was guilty of keeping score and being mad at him when he didn't meet what I felt were obvious and righteous expectations. And if I'm honest, this came from feelings of shame and jealousy. I*

felt shame because I wasn't out working, and I felt as though nothing I did at home was important; and jealousy because he got to go out and DO something with his day instead of being STUCK at home with children.

"Because I started listening to you, Dr. Laura, I changed that mind-set and the keeping score stopped. And we are both happier for that. I was making myself crazy with it. Although my marriage wasn't in trouble, had I not changed my thinking—it would have been."

When confronted by a score-keeping spouse, either being hard on themselves as inadequate—or puffing themselves up as superior—I try to help them eliminate that destructive thinking by asking the following question: "Who is more important? The pilot of a fighter jet, or the person whose sole job it is to put that last screw into the wing?"

Believe it or not, the typical answer is "The fighter pilot!" I tell them, "WRONG!" They are aghast and argumentative. "Look at the training, talent, education, responsibility . . . how could the pilot not be the most important?"

"Simple," I say, "the pilot can't get the plane off the ground to run his mission without that one screw being properly placed and secured." A quiet "Oh" is usually the reply.

The romantic notion of marriage meaning you become ONE is more than just a platitude. All the many things that must be done to support you both so that you can function as a person is TEAMWORK. And no part is more important than any other part because all the small parts add up to the UNION which should be the most important concept in your mind and heart.

Let's just say that you both want to go to the movies after you have dinner at home. Who should put the dishes in the dishwasher? Do you wait to see if the other will do it? Do you do it in anger? Do you nag or threaten your beloved to do it?

If the goal *is* the movies together, then the goal is *not* who is subservient and who is superior by virtue of who takes care of the dishes. Maybe one of you says, "I'll get the dishes cleared away, how about you warm up the car?" or "Which do you want, rinsing or dishwasher?" or "You've had a tough day. Let me get the dishes while you take a warm shower before we go out." See? This changes everything from competition to collaboration. Which do you believe is more loving?

Some of you are going to have a hard time with this because, frankly, you are control freaks. Debbie has something to say about that!

> *"I went into my second marriage wanting him to cater to me and to make my happy. My husband just gave and gave and I took and took until it became real clear to me how horrid I was being.*
>
> *"I was a control freak used to doing everything my way. I was always pointing out some way in which he had let me down—much to my shame. Now I consider him first and try to give more than I get. Marriage has made me a better person in that it has made me WAY less selfish and argumentative than I was when we married.*
>
> *"Being married means someone's always got my back, having my best friend around all the time, great sex, and more personal growth than I could have imagined or admitted I needed! The biggest mistake most couples make is not understanding that the most important thing isn't 'me,' it's 'us.' "*

The most important concept in Debbie's letter is the understanding that your spouse is not your enemy. I think that needs repeating: your spouse is not your enemy. Yet so many people treat their spouses as though they were really their reincarnated mean parent or competitive sibling and they lie in wait for the assault to begin.

Another listener wrote that he treated his wife as though she were his sibling with whom he had to compete for an imagined lack of resources and seek validation through "being right." He feared that if he was found to be flawed, wrong, or imperfect, that his wife wouldn't love him, so he got really defensive when criticized or when he imagined he'd done something wrong. When they had a disagreement, instead of being her partner and working to find a common ground toward a resolution, he got defensive and gave tit-for-tat arguments to prove that he was more long suffering and more hard working and more important than she.

Sound familiar?

His parents divorced when he and his sibling were very young. His parents got into their own love lives with various partners and his dad, between girlfriends and work, was never around. His sibling had learning disorder issues and got a lot of attention. Add all of this up and instead of his becoming a grown man, taking care of his woman, he was a little boy hungry for love and validation, and hypersensitive to even the thought of losing it at any particular moment.

"Yes, I believe that these behaviors are fixable. Usually when I act out inappropriately, I figure it out later and get embarrassed and apologize to my spouse. More and more I am getting better at being able to stop myself. I use some of the things you've said on your program as a chant to keep me from following my knee-jerk response, such as, 'She is not the enemy,' and 'No one is loved because they're perfect.' "

When you walk into a room and are introduced to a new

person, you put out your hand immediately to shake hands, don't you? Sure you do, it's just polite. It is amazing, though, how many of you spouse-types don't put out your hand to your spouse unless he/she does it first.

Elizabeth wrote that she and her husband have been married almost two decades and are more in love than ever because ten years ago she realized that she was responsible for the chasm between them—a chasm getting wider and wider every day. She admitted to mirroring his behavior toward her, meaning that she behaved lovingly only when she *perceived* he was behaving lovingly toward her. She did things for him only when she *perceived* he was doing things for her. She complimented him only when she *perceived* he was doing things for her.

"As soon as I behaved AS IF . . . and took the lead in loving him—the change in his attitude and behaviors toward me was almost overnight!"

The emphasis on "perceived" is because the mix between reality and our sensitivities often cancels out the good we could be enjoying. One woman called me to complain that her husband never said loving things to her. However she did recount in passing that he went out at five A.M. to scrape the ice off her windshield and warm up her car so she would be comfortable going to work. I asked her, "Isn't that the loudest 'I love you!' a woman has ever heard?"

Don't even think about keeping score with who does what; **Do** keep in sight of what the goal in your marriage is: peace and happiness.

Don't compete with your beloved for who is more important; **Do** spend every possible moment telling your spouse he/she is the most important part of your life.

Don't withhold love or affection because of some perceived slight—or even an actual slight; **Do** remember that a cherished spouse will "slight" you less.

Love Alert! When I take a shower, I love the bathroom to be totally dark so I can just relax and luxuriate in the hot water. One night my husband came in to use his sink and he turned the light on over that area. I opened the shower door and asked him to turn off the light because I needed this quiet time. He was momentarily bugged because he was trying to find something. He turned off the light and left the bathroom.

Now this could have turned into an "I have my stuff to do and don't interfere with me" competitive moment. But it didn't 'cause he's a good guy.

The next night, while I was again in the shower, I had left one of the lights on and just didn't want to leave the warm shower to turn it off. Humpff. Then I noticed that my husband came into the bathroom, saw/heard the shower, went and turned off the light, and silently left. That is an "I love you" moment. Learn to hear/see these!

SHOW ME THE MONEY!

They say that money and sex are the two biggest causes of divorce. I don't think so. I believe that they are merely more obvious symptoms of the lack of ability and willingness to desire to make your spouse's, your beloved's, your woman's/man's life worth living. Instead your focus is your fears and immature/neurotic needs that result in a desperate attempt to control in order to keep safe from imagined dangers from your childhood.

Consequently some of you are cheap and miserly and some of you spend like crazy. Money becomes a means by which you attempt to solve your emotional problems from your childhood. Perhaps you spend over the budget because that is how you deal with anxieties about your own value or depression over your self-obsession with looks, smarts, happiness, or whatever. Perhaps you hoard money and control expenditures because that is how you deal with anxieties about loss, loneliness, and failure.

You may point a finger at your spouse, condemning them for not being as responsible or generous as you, and you may be absolutely right! However it is interesting that you made the choice to marry and form a household with them in spite of knowing about their financial behaviors and perspectives. Once done it is important to work *with* them on compromise, instead of *against* them with anger.

One recent example from my radio program might help in this regard. A woman called very upset because she has built up a lot of credit card debt with spending on household things and stuff for the kids. She didn't know what to do at this point, and was obviously too scared of the consequences and reaction to tell her husband.

Her husband is very organized and meticulous about bills and budgets and hasn't at all respected her as a partner in these areas as she is such a "free spirit" about money. Basically it made her feel like she's the teenager and he's the parent, doling out an allowance totally at his whim.

I told her to go to him that very night and present the bills with an apology. She was to tell him that she was treated as a child and sank to the occasion and behaved like a rebellious child and spent behind his back. She was to clarify that she did not spend frivolously on "stupid girl stuff," but instead on reasonable things for the home and family. She was not to yell, cry, attack, or argue. When she finished her story, she was to stay quiet until his reaction was over. At that point she was to say, "I appreciate that you are more experienced and knowledgeable about family budgets, but I feel left out of our life in this area and you must feel like you don't have a partner you can trust and count on. This is sad for both of us. Here is my suggestion: I will work up a weekly/ monthly budget for all those things I need for us all and after we agree on this, you can place that amount in a checking account. I will then work from that. Each month we'll go over what has transpired—maybe even savings!—and we'll discuss any changes we think ought to be made."

She was to then hug and kiss him, and say that she's looking forward to reducing this source of tension between them so that they both could feel more safe and affectionate with each other.

She called back several days later to say that she "blew his mind" with how grown-up, responsible, brave, complimentary, and sensitive he saw her being and that things were working out well so far.

What I worried about was how emotionally constipated he might be, which would clearly get in the way of his being open to sharing responsibility and control. Obviously she approached him with enough sensitivity to his sensitivities that he came out of himself.

The aforementioned "constipation" reference is generally a result of "starvation" as a child: emotional and/or virtual. "*I was OBSESSED with not being poor*," wrote Douglas. "*I grew up in a difficult situation.*" Sometimes folks who, as children, were not treated with open love and affection, or whose families suffered great financial hardships (due to circumstance or irresponsibility) will find themselves hoarding money and affection/attention. The cure to deficits in one's childhood is *not* hoarding; the cure is to become a virtual wellspring of what you missed. That's where the relief comes from.

Please, you must remember your ultimate goal: **peace and happiness.** And that doesn't mean you repair your childhood struggles and dramas by dragging your spouse into a reenactment of your upbringing that you will make damn sure "goes your way" better than your childhood did!

Repeat after me: peace and happiness, peace and happiness, peace and happiness! Good. Now keep in mind that peace and happiness cannot be arm-wrestled, demanded, bullied, or threatened into being. Peace and happiness are the results of **loving and giving.**

Rick discovered the blessings accrued by giving. He and his wife adopted a two-month-old. He hadn't wanted to have children because his wife was working and he believed he couldn't afford to have her stay home—which he knew was best for the child. He loved his life the way it was because they did whatever they wanted without worrying about money. But once this beautiful child came into their home, Rick realized that there was more to life than his selfish desires.

"Every time I looked at my son I would think of my second mom, Dr. Laura, telling me to have my wife stay home. I would tell my wife about Dr. Laura's haunting voice in my head all the time.

"I had this investment account set aside with enough money to pay off both cars and our credit cards. This would enable my

wife to stay home while I would still have to work some over-time to make it work. At first I fought tooth and nail to keep my wife working.

"My wife kept telling me to call Dr. Laura to ask what she would say about cashing in the account to afford her to stay home. I dreaded making the call because I knew the answer Dr. Laura would give me and I didn't want to sound like all those other callers, saying, 'Yeah, I know, I know.'

"I bit the bullet and cashed in the account. I know it was the right decision but that doesn't make it any less scary. I have faith in God and I know things will be fine. I really appreciate all your motherly advice!"

I have been growing in my dismay at the number of women who don't value the magnificent gift of motherly attention to a child and the number of men who don't value the magnificent gift of fatherly support. It seems we've grown a few generations of males, not men. A man does what it takes to protect and provide for his woman and children. Too many males today sound more like Rick used to sound: "I like my things! We both need to work so I can enjoy my things!"

Lately I've gotten calls from a large number of women curious as to my take on whether their husbands should hold out for a job they love and are "happy" with, or a job that takes care of business for the family. These wives feel guilty that their husbands might not be "happy," as though happiness were the greatest good, and that it could only be obtained through "having."

I tell them all that *real men* are happy to be able to take care of their families no matter what they have to suffer to do it. Most of the time, these women callers are astonished at that answer. I refer them to history, when men sustained themselves through terrible hardships but retained the pride of knowing that their sacrifices were the strength of the family's survival.

One such woman, Bridgitte, wrote:

"The first mistake I made in my marriage was not anticipating and implementing a financial plan to stay at home with my children. Before marriage, I never expected to want to stay at home, and while dating I never voiced this possibility.

"Now that I have been home for almost three years, dealing with monumental resentment from my husband and him feeling unloved because I've let him have all financial responsibility, my husband is asking on a daily basis if my daughter is worth all of the strain."

Frankly if Bridgitte puts her daughter in day care and goes to work full-time, she will definitely solve the money problem— but the marriage will be lost because her respect for her man will be gone, and her guilt at sacrificing her daughter will eat at her heart.

It is not unusual for educated women such as Bridgitte to come to realize that a more traditional marital approach (one parent nurturing children; other parent slaying dragons) is superior to dueling careers and neglected children; exhausted, frazzled wives and alienated/emasculated husbands. As I tell women ambivalent about this issue: "You can work outside the home when your child is in kindergarten—as long as you leave for work after the child goes to school and are home when your child hits the front door for a mommy hug!"

Bridgitte continued:

"My problem was thinking that most aspects of a traditional marriage were absurd (i.e., the man as the primary breadwinner)

but now I find myself in the . . . position of being educated and wondering if parenting is a significant enough contribution— yearning for most aspects of a traditional marriage. I know it's not too late to make some changes!"

There is another side to this issue. Ervin had listened intently to my many provocative lectures on a "real man," and reflected on a "real woman":

"You keep saying a real man brings home the money so the mother can stay home with the children. What you fail to say is it takes a real woman to take the money and use it responsibly to take care of the family. Without her working to manage the money wisely your concept will not work.

"The mom needs to be conservative or it will be a lost cause. Please stop blaming it on the man for mom working. For me and others I know mom wants more and more and decides on her own to get a job to buy her luxuries and the man still spends his money on the family bills."

Fair enough and well said!

Nonetheless research shows that women still tend to prefer men who are breadwinners, whom they can consider intellectually superior, and who can physically protect them. Women tend to respect more and be sexually attracted to men who can take care of them.

Don't ever make money the measure of the importance of either one of you; **Do** think of money as the joint air you breathe . . . use it wisely and enjoy it.

Don't allow your insecurities to rule how money is saved and spent; **Do** remember that having your spouse know that you are joined as a team, struggling together, reaping the rewards together is, for you, a wonderful blessing.

Don't use spending or hoarding money as a means of punishment or control; **Do** try to balance your whims, desires, and needs with a responsible sense of awareness that you both benefit from or are hurt by money problems.

Love Alert! How money is earned and spent is a subject that needs calm, frank, and constant attention. I think a good rule is that for the big things (and each marriage at different times must determine the dividing line for "big") there ought to be a conference and a mutual decision. If an agreement cannot be made the "NO" wins. It behooves spouses to realize that when you thwart the reasonable desires of the other too often, you win the battle but lose the peace and happiness.

An important part of every budget is "swing" money, that is, money that each can splurge or save without the big discussion. It is gratifying for each to feel some freedom for the silly things.

CHILDREN IN THE PICTURE

How is it that something that can't walk or talk, much less roll over on its own or even use the channel changer, can RULE the universe? A child changes everything. The biggest mistakes that spouses make when children arrive are (1) getting themselves all consumed and emotionally spent with the children, (2) having dueling parenting styles, and (3) abdication of parental leadership responsibilities because they want to be liked.

The first problem results in the spouse and the marriage being abandoned and neglected, which is sad and foolish because if children are your main concern, then keeping their home safe, secure, warm, and functional should be your first motivation.

The second mistake results in parents not working as a team by becoming combatants, which lets the children rule the household; did you ever read *Lord of the Flies*?

The third mistake results in out-of-control children, causing problems and bringing a tremendous amount of unhappiness to a marriage that cannot be endured because the marriage has ceased being a partnership in child-rearing.

One specific area with built-in aggravation is a stepfamily situation. Generally the stepparent has no power with step-children and is saddled with the animus of the prior marriage, especially on issues of discipline, planning, privacy, money, expectations, and so forth. Second marriages with children have a higher divorce rate than first marriages—I always beg people to wait until their kids are grown before dating and remarrying. Of course, even when kids are grown, one has to find a prospective mate who isn't hostile about sharing time with the reality of extended nonbiological family.

The central point though is that spouses not lose each other, swallowed up by the reality of the needs of children. Michel admitted,

> *"After we had kids and they were doing sports, dance, and piano, my wife gave me zero time. I noticed women at work and starting giving them compliments, spending more time talking to them and looking at every girl that caught my eye. I was starting to think about other women more than my wife and it scared me. I sat my wife down and told her about this and how I felt. My wife is a good woman and she agreed that the kids had come first—and said she was going to change. And she did!*

"Our marriage changed and was awesome! A month after this, I remember thinking that there is not a woman more beautiful than my wife. I don't even look anymore because I am so satisfied with her. It's easy to keep a man that worships you—just make him feel like a man."

Many women call me to complain that their husbands need to understand that they now share their attention with the children. What I reflect back in most of these calls is that the term "sharing" suggests that there is attention for them; that's often not the case. Many woman callers, when presented by me with their virtual elimination of any recognition, respect, or attention to their husband's needs and desires for them, say, "Yeah, I know . . . BUT . . ." "But" has no place in that sentence if a marriage is going to thrive. There is not a woman alive who would tolerate a man paying all his attention to his child and telling his wife, "Sorry, you'll just have to fend for yourself because I'm tired and have nothing left over for you."

And that brings me perhaps to one central issue: TIME. You can't do and have it all simultaneously. You can't even have it all sequentially—unless of course you're immortal. I can't tell you how many men and women call and tell me that they *know* they should spend more time together, but what with feeding the kids dinner and putting them to bed (after the children have had a full day of day care or day care and school), a full-time job and full-time work . . . there's nothing left. NO KIDDING!? I usually ask these people, "Why did you bother to marry? Why bother having kids?" Their answer is, "Because I wanted to have a family." My response? "HAVE a family, like a possession, or actually BE family, by sacrificing for their sake . . . and ultimately, yours?" This usually engenders pure quiet.

Don't overbook children's activities—it isn't good for them and it eliminates family and intimate time; **Do** make sure that you take time every day to make your beloved feel beloved and special.

Don't assume you are always right about every issue of parenting; your spouse's experiences and ideas may be different, but different is not automatically wrong or bad; **Do** defer to your spouse on discipline or decision making with respect to the kids—it shows the children that you are a team and it'll make your spouse feel respected. Remember, there are many roads to Rome.

Don't try to make your child your best friend or put your child in the position of having to choose between the two of you; **Do** make every attempt possible to engage your spouse in decision making so that when you present something to your kids (punishment, rules, etc.), it is from US.

Love Alert! Even if you didn't discuss the particulars of raising children before you married (tsk tsk)—it is never too late. How 'bout the two of you sit down and talk about the blessings and problems of your respective childhoods. Then openly and courageously reveal how you think your own brand of parenting is more about your own early childhood pain, and less about the best interests of the family. When each of you is being open, the other needs to be physically (hold hands) and emotionally supportive. In this way you will both get rid of baggage and free yourselves up to enjoy and improve in your parenting skills with the *help* instead of the *argument* of each other. Parenting classes taken together will be a big help. Get out of yourself and into each other! Think of the peace and happiness of knowing that even at your worst (admitting failures and weaknesses) your beloved loves you even more and feels that much closer.

Don't abuse your children by using them as a safety spacer between you and what you're not comfortable with in your spouse. Yes, that's right, that is child abuse. For the sake of the children, as well as your own peace and happiness, your marriage must come first—NO EXCUSES. When it is time to give your adult child the pink slip on his/her life, do it and fill that empty nest with marital love and new adventures.

Chapter 5

To Hell and Back

To Hell: "*We never used the word divorce, but one day we sat on either side of the bed with our backs to each other. We were, for lack of a better word, tired,*" wrote Benjamin, a listener.

They each asked each other, "What are we going to do?" They each responded, "I'm not going anywhere."

And Back: "*We faced each other, lay on the bed and began talking about all of our fears, frustrations and hurts. We found that we had the same concerns about one another. We cried, we talked, we kissed, and we held each other all night.*

"*That was ten years ago and here we are approaching our 25th anniversary in December.*"

I believe the folks who know the most and the best about how to stay married *well*, are those who have gone to hell and found a way to come back. Platitudes and lovely stories are inspiring and educational, but when a marriage has gotten to the point of hate and terminal hurt and the man and woman find a way back to each other, past all that, that is some kind of miracle we all have to know more about. It is these marriages that demonstrate above all others how sacred and special the marital covenant is, for only those things that are deeply meaningful are worth fighting for.

I am impressed that anyone fights for their marriage at all. The liberal mentality supporting a total lack of structure for people (hooking up, shacking up, out-of-wedlock children by choice, abortions for convenience, promiscuity no longer a dirty word) certainly works against especially younger people discovering and appreciating the blessings of having someone in your life as part of a covenant. With so many of their parents divorcing—often multiple times—young people are afraid of hurt and loss so they "play" with intimacy without really risking much in the hope that they can create "safe love," only to discover that such a situation doesn't exist and that they feel desperately lonely.

There isn't much in our culture (media and neighborhood) that portrays traditional love and marriage in hopeful ways, nor is their much support for those who attempt to venture into a committed relationship. Largely people are left floundering or using personal fantasies.

Carrie, another listener, described her two-year marriage as very unhappy and she thought it was time to get out rather than prolong the misery. She had had dreams and fantasies about the "perfect life," an expectation that wasn't being met in spite of the fact that they were such good friends. He didn't want a divorce but she just *wanted it to be done so I could move on—so I filed for divorce.*"

Their basic friendship kept them talking and discussing their thoughts and feelings. He even helped her move into her new apartment so she could be on her own—for the first time in her life! They discovered that they were having a better time together separated than when they were married. They became better friends and better communicators as they shared their thoughts and feelings without the rancor of their ill-conceived notions about marriage being perfect all on its own; two people, just add water and stir.

"Ultimately we realized [all we suffered] *was something we had to go through to get where we needed to be—to understand what we had been blind to before. We will be celebrating our ten-year anniversary this year. It is not that life has been easy, but we certainly have a greater appreciation for marriage, the commitment and savoring the good, bad, and in between times of a relationship."*

Of course it is instant disaster, not instant happiness, when two people come together, each with their own notions of how it is going to be—almost on its own—when they marry. Many people perceive marriage as a kind of sauna, you go in and the heat does something to you while you are passive. What Carrie and her husband happily discovered was that a good marriage is all about "doing" something, instead of expecting something. When both spouses understand that—it is a beautiful thing.

Lori wrote that she had filed for divorce five years ago after a sixteen-year marriage. She related not being able to bear another day of being treated as the least important person in the universe. She described her husband as self-centered, chauvinistic, disconnected from her and everyone else to the point that all that mattered to him was his work and the accolades everyone gave him for being so technically smart and valuable to his company. She described how he often volunteered to be told how great he was.

"He left me alone to deal with anything difficult like my mother's and two brothers' untimely deaths. What was important to me just didn't matter to him. The home repairs were neglected to the point of embarrassment. I was married but very alone. I became an angry wife with much resentment toward him."

She went to a marriage counselor, who affirmed that she

had a right to be angry and a right to be happy. She thought
that to be happy she had to leave that mess and start anew with
a person who was willing to grow with her and share her values—and this marriage seemed hopeless.

They spent $5,000 each for divorce attorneys and the real
fighting began, with depositions and court appearances. They
were still under one roof and the tensions were unbearable.
And then . . .

> *"My husband came to me in tears one day during this time
> and said that he came to the realization that this was it, every-
> thing we built together would be gone, our four sons at the
> time—between 11 and 16 years of age—would be crushed and
> broken just like the homes we were both raised in. He promised
> to do whatever it took to repair and rebuild our relationship.*
>
> *"I told him that we'd have to live in a cared-for home that
> I could be proud of and that I'd have to be treated like I WAS
> IMPORTANT! HE WANTED TO BE ACCEPTED
> and have a loving wife and a peaceful home. We both promised
> to do our best.*
>
> *"Today, and each day, we work on bringing our best selves
> into this family, and we have, for the most part, succeeded. I
> decided that no matter what transpired, I would not lose con-
> trol over my emotions anymore. Our home is peaceful and I'm
> happy (by choice) and our boys are secure and loved by us both
> each day.*
>
> *"I know we are doing the right thing for our children. Once
> they're raised, I'll look at our relationship closer and see if we
> can extend our commitment to stay true to our vows. He still
> has issues that he doesn't address, but I have accepted them for
> now. As you say, Dr. Laura, I've stopped fighting them. A*

two-parent home where the adults demonstrate love, respect,
and compassion and show the value of family are what's most
important to me. I'm very thankful we both found the strength
to keep it together."

Lori's story brings up an important point—which is difficult
for most people: when you know the other person's core drive,
main issue, biggest need—don't fight it or criticize it . . . work
with it. Lori needed to feel important. Lori's husband needed
to be approved of, and be seen as special. As they both came
from broken homes where parents had their own problems,
their biggest "need" derived from their biggest "loss" as children. When we spend our adult years trying to fill the space
that should have been filled as a child, we end up ignoring our
spouses and being in competition with their needs.

Lori finally recognized and toned down her angry responses,
and that made her husband turn less to work and volunteering
to get attention and approval. When Lori's husband realized
that Lori leaving him was his ultimate worst nightmare—
withdrawal of approval—he fought to do what she needed (to
feel important to him) in order to regain her approval. Instead
of fighting each other's core need, they turned to feeding that
need; in doing so, they both became better people and better
spouses. Funny how that works out!

Chris and his wife were also at the brink of divorce. He'd
discovered his wife's affair and had told her from the beginning
of their relationship that that was the one thing he definitely
would not tolerate. They had two children, thirteen and fifteen, and a twenty-year marriage. He was planning his exit
strategy when he met three men who had divorced in the last
one to five years.

"Not one of them was better off now than before. All had bad times with the split family hurting the kids. All were financially worse off than before. Not one of them had anything good to say about their life post-divorce. Bitterness, loneliness, emptiness, and loss were evident in their conversations—besides, I calculated that the divorce would cost me about $60,000!"

Chris brought up a very important point: most people look at divorce as the saving grace without examining it more deeply. When I was in training as a marriage and family therapist, I remember reading a research paper stating that upward of 75 percent of divorces were unnecessary and that most people did not report being happier after their divorce. The reasons are obvious: loneliness, financial problems, children's pain and acting out, visitation issues, dealing with the ex's new relationships and children, greater daily burdens not shared, and so forth.

Chris's wife went into intensive therapy to deal with her personal problems with a "bad-dad" hangover (controlling, unloving, put-downs, etc.) and followed through on trust through verification (cell phone bills, e-blaster computer reports, lots of touching base during the day, etc.). *"It is now 1.5 years after the explosion and we are more in love now than in many years. It was hard to grow back the trust but the decision to put 150% back into making this thing work was hard and painful—but oh so worth it!"*

One of the best descriptions of surviving hell and coming back in a marriage was sent to me by a firefighter, Thomas. He wrote that he had a revelation about marriage and divorce one day while actually fighting a fire. He talked about the claustrophobic feeling a firefighter gets from being hot because of the fire and the heavy protective gear they wear.

"It's the same feeling we get when we're standing in the sun on a hot summer day when you're wearing a hot, heavy sweater. Intolerable! The only reason wearing heavy clothing in the summer becomes intolerable is because we have the choice not to. If the choice is not there, it somehow becomes bearable—because you endure.

"In firefighting, I have to wear a heavy turnout coat and pants in the heat. I never get the TEAR THIS STUFF OFF NOW OR I'M GONNA DIE feeling. That fact that I'm baking never even occurs to me because there's nothing I can do about it—taking the stuff off is not an option.

"Marriage and divorce is the same way. So many people are getting divorces because they consider it an option. Even if it's a last option, they will still turn to it when things get too 'hot.' Marriage is very tolerable when you don't keep your eye on the EXIT door.

"In my marriage we don't even consider divorce as an option, so there is no temptation to take that route, and things we experience become tolerable. There are times divorce has entered my head, but I just throw it out and know I have to work on making things 'cooler,' not just running from the heat.

"Life is hot. Heat is everywhere."

Life *is* hot and heat *is* everywhere, so think ahead when divorce seems the only solution for right now.

One day Kory's wife dropped the "divorce" bomb on him and he was even more stunned to realize that he wasn't too disappointed with her decision. After about seven hours of discussing what their living and custody arrangements were going to be, they came to the realization that neither of them really wanted to be apart, but had just forgotten to put in the effort needed to keep a marriage strong. *"How easily we do forget."*

It is four years since that day, and their marriage is still going strong. He compares his sometimes "distant from her feelings" to his truck's gas gauge; the feelings are letting him know that his tank is getting low, "*and only I can fill it. The way that I fill it is to show my wife how much she really means to me. The more I give the more I get. As time goes by I feel that empty feeling less and less. If I remember any advice that my dad gave me, it was to never let your gas light come on. It is just as easy to fill the top half of your tank as it is to fill the bottom.*"

And smarter, don't you think?

"THE BRINK OF DIVORCE"… A BLESSING IN DISGUISE?

Patricia and her husband had a long history of infertility problems. After years of treatments and surgeries for both of them, she had three consecutive miscarriages. The fertility problems and the miscarriages strained their marriage to the brink of divorce.

> "*I was wrapped up in my own self-pity and neglected to love and nurture my marriage through this hellish time in our lives. I know that most of my feelings were a result of my wacky post-pregnancy hormones, and my own grief over the death of our babies. I have always wanted children and I thought I should set my husband free so he could marry a woman who could give him what I could not. Yes, this was very childish and stupid on my part. This was a miserable time in our lives, and I did not think our marriage would survive the immense heartache we were both experiencing.*
>
> "*Then, after much prayer, we were finally able to scrape ourselves out of our grief and get back to living the life God meant*

us to live. We finally realized our commitment to each other, and happiness in our marriage took precedence over the heartache trying to conceive children brought us. We simply decided that having children naturally was not worth our marriage. We do hope to adopt some day."

She went on to say that she believes this very dark time in their lives was a **blessing in disguise,** because they now feel that if they could work through this, they can work through anything. It has made a bond between them that would never had been there if they had taken the easier way out and called it quits. It taught them how to work out their problems instead of pulling inside themselves and away from each other. No matter what challenge confronts them in the future, this experience taught them, promised them, that they could get through it . . . together.

DON'T WANT TO HURT THE KIDS

Conventional wisdom has it that having children generally puts a strain on a marriage. That is true. However there is another side to that story.

Harrison and his wife were newly married. She was an airline attendant with a solid financial base and had even purchased a home with a female colleague; she was used to security. Harrison was an entrepreneur who had just sold a business and was revving up to start a new one having found an opportunity in another state. They moved states, had the financial strain of starting a new business, and then she became pregnant. Things were getting out of hand since she was pregnant, not used to debt, and uncomfortable with the prospect of purchasing a business with debt. It was getting bad.

After she gave birth, something incredible happened.

> *"With the addition of our new family member, we both dedicated our life to her. The pressures of the proposed business purchase seemed to melt away as we concentrated on our daughter. For my wife it was the 'best' experience ever, even for a girl that never aspired to have children.*
>
> *"Now in our late 50s we are closer than ever and the reason is the joy of our now two children. It has given us the* **direction** *and* **purpose** *that otherwise would have been lacking in our relationship."*

I believe that people mature with marriage (or at least have the opportunity to) and become unselfish with parenting (or at least have the opportunity to). It is not that people exist only for their children—they shouldn't—it is that they see a point to life past their own self-importance and gratification.

Having children is a monumental responsibility, and it is that recognition that often pulls people up short when they consider dumping their marriage. John wrote that he and his wife had been happily married for six years when they ran into some severe problems. It was a combination of his wife lying to him about finances, and his own need to look for something beyond his marriage to make his life more "exciting."

> *"I had worked my way up to saying that the only recourse was for us was divorce and to get away from each other. What happened to stop it? Three simple words: Maggie, Emily, and Joey . . . my kids. I could not do this (divorce) to them. I was responsible for their lives and even though I 'thought' I might be happier without my wife, I knew I wouldn't be happier without them.*

"This doesn't sound romantic or anything special, but it made me stop to look at my life and my wife. The kids made me stop before doing something stupid, but afterward I saw that I truly love my wife; we have good days and bad days, but mostly we just have days together."

I always try to remind callers with children threatening divorce that it won't be just about them and their spouse—it'll be about destroying their children's lives; unless the situation is dangerous or destructive, it should be endured for their sakes. And you know what? When you're there because you've endured, wonderful things can happen—which will never if you leave.

Karl wrote about his experience with his parents when he was ten on a summer's evening in 1978. The family had just come home from a wonderful day, or so he thought. As he played with his new record player and headphones, he was unaware that his parents were in the living room having a bitter argument. Suddenly his father burst into his room and said, "Come in here, son, we need to talk to you." He was annoyed, having to turn off *The Muppet Movie,* and went into the living room. He noticed his mother was in tears and his dad was very serious.

"That's when he hit me with it—'Your mom and I are getting separated.' What? After what was a perfect day in a kid's life, my folks drop this bombshell on me? No. NO! I wasn't going to let them ruin my day (more important to me at the time than the implications of their actions on the rest of my life).

" 'No,' I said with tears starting to well up in my eyes, 'you can't do this to me. Do you know what this is going to do to me? I'll never get to see you together again. We'll never

*be a family again. YOU CAN'T STAY TOGETHER
FOR ME?' "*

His parents started to backpedal by assuring him that this
would only be a trial run, and after a few weeks, they'd probably get back together again.

*"Well, then why leave at all, if you're going to get back together in
a few weeks? Make it work. Aren't I worth it? Keep trying!"*

His parents reassured him that they would. Satisfied, he
went back to Miss Piggy and the Muppet gang.

His parents will be celebrating their forty-ninth wedding anniversary, and he modestly assumes credit for making it happen!

Oh that more children could/would fight back in such a
way.

Most of the time, getting a divorce is just quitting.

As Ann, another listener, wrote, there were three things she
knew she had to do to save her marriage from her deep resentment and insecurity:

> *"1. I had to remember why I married my husband—
>   which may not have been because he was such a great
>   provider, but because of his gentle manner, complete
>   emotional support of me, his incredible integrity and
>   dependability—all of which were still there.*
> *"2. I had to realize my fears and insecurities were exag-
>   gerated because of my childhood and that these were
>   my issues and not him doing something wrong.*
> *"3. The greatest lesson I learned and try to tell oth-
>   ers is that marriage is like learning 100 Russian
>   words. You can say, 'I can't learn Russian, it's too
>   hard.' But the FACT is that you could if you truly
>   were committed. Each morning you could learn one*

*word—after a while, it gets easier and the words can
become sentences.*

*"Marriage takes work; committing to it each morning keeps
it from getting away from us and it keeps getting easier.*
*"The greatest reward is when we ask our three-year-old who
he wants to read to him and tuck him in and he says, 'I want
Mommy on this side and I want Papa on this side.' "*

Commitment has great rewards, especially in the eyes and
hearts of your children.

I'M LEAVING OR YOU'RE OUT!

It is sad but true that sometimes the camel has to completely
drop down dead before some folks are motivated to be and do
better in their marriages.

Jim reported that his crisis came twenty years into the marriage. His sisters and friends kept saying that he had the patience
of Job in letting his wife run over him. His wife was very inse-
cure because of a terrible childhood. She was controlling and
unloving. He was simply determined never to let the marriage
break up while the kids needed them both. He endured.

One day while they were shopping, his wife saw a friend of
hers approaching and immediately put her arm around Jim's
waist. He was really irritated that she did that as a "show" for
her friend; she hadn't hugged him in ten years!

When they got to the car, he realized he had reached his
limit, and said,

*"Honey, you had no business putting your arm around me
that way. If you cannot show me affection in our home, then you*

*need not try faking it in public. You seem to never find anything
I do as acceptable or good and I seem to be a great aggravation to
you. Life is simply too short for us to be miserable any longer. I
am therefore going to release you from your vows to me. I simply
love you too much to see you in this agony any longer.*

*"Since I seem to be the source of that misery, we will part.
I'll be packing as soon as we get home. Perhaps you will then
be able to find another man who will be able to let you be
happy."*

She sat quietly all the way home. He held to his promise
and began packing. She walked around the house for a time
and watched him. When he began putting his tools in his truck
and spoke to her about finances, she broke down and began
really crying . . . and promising she would change.

She did change and they continued their marriage.

*"Sure, there were stumblings and slips and occasional spats but
we worked through them. She slowly began showing me more
respect and honor, and over the next few years things became
much better. We now have three grandkids, married 34 years,
and our home is continual peace. In fact, today we are as happy
as we have ever been in our entire lives."*

I always remind people to never use leaving as a manipulation; it is an ultimatum of the sort that must never be made
except in earnest. Leaving should be the very last option.
While it is true that many people who won't see they need
to change or say/think they cannot change, make huge leaps
when confronted with the ultimate rejection, it is also true that
some people give lip service to changing once the nest gets
secure again.

Nonetheless "leaving" is often a powerful "rebooting" of the marriage, reminding each person that they have obligations to the other, not just a right to expectations for themselves.

Nicole described her marriage as a perpetual fight.

"We didn't even want to be in the same room as each other. It took my husband leaving and going to a hotel room to really hit us that this was it!

"That night he called me on his cell and we talked for a long time—and for the first time I think we actually heard each other. Funny how it took us being on a phone and not in the same room to be able to get our points across.

"He then came home and we just simply started to show each other affection. We knew that we had to work on our issues but that they would not be resolved overnight. We also knew that we once had a very passionate relationship and that we were once very much in love—and the number one reason is we had two boys who needed their mom AND their dad.

"The more affection we gave each other and the increase in sex actually helped us. He started to change and so did I. We just reminded each other why we fell in love and what it felt like and that helped us talk nicer and open up a lot more to each other I can now again say that I am so in love with my husband and he is with me too!!"

Many people get it backward: they think they have to talk everything out, resolve everything completely, and see a ton of concrete changes before they will *maybe* feel in love again. Actually the compassionate, sensitive, and loving *gestures* have to come *before* the feelings. Generally actions drag feelings along and not the opposite. Husbands and wives must treat each other with the tender, loving regard they once had in order to reinitialize positive feelings about their spouse. The more you *think* and *do* loving things, the more you will feel loving.

Does that mean you're being phony? No. It means you're thinking positively and making an investment based on earlier wonderful returns.

As Michelle offered, *"I think the biggest mistake people make in a marriage is forgetting that you can still be girlfriend and boyfriend. We tend to treat each other more like roommates because we get comfortable. We don't give enough compliments and praise. We let our bodies go and think that the other person will love us no matter what. We stop experimenting with new things together and settle into the same old routines. Continuing these activities once married helps keep things together, especially when the times get tough."*

And this is twice as important when you're on the brink of divorce. Actually Michelle and her husband, both of whom came from divorced families, had been divorced for nine months, ostensibly due to his infidelity. Once apart they realized the magnitude of what they had given up. They were so motivated to not continue their family divorce traditions that they used that energy to break through their fears and really open up to each other. After agreeing to care for one another more tenderly, and never to bring up the past (which can't be changed) as punishment or leverage in an argument, they remarried.

WHAT? IT ISN'T SUPPOSED TO BE ALL ABOUT ME?

The number one most difficult task in the entire world is to think outside the box—when it is yourself that is the box! Don't take it personally; to some degree, this is true for everyone. Your thoughts and feelings are immediately accessible to you—you can know the thoughts and feelings of your spouse only if they tell you. But if they tell you and you refuse to listen, denounce their truths and perspectives, deny any culpability for their feelings, or excuse yourself from having to respond lovingly to their needs because you have hurts too—then, simply, you lose them—even if they are still under the same roof.

I had one such call recently from a woman with two small children who wanted to know what she should do with her husband. It seems he's told her that he needs more attention from her. She refused to admit that his request was reasonable, because in her view she gave him sufficient attention. It is difficult with two small children and a trying day to always be sensitive and accommodating to one's spouse; however, the spouse becomes hopeless when their plea is dismissed.

Try as I might, I couldn't get through to her. She and I ended with this sad exchange:

Caller: Well, I need time for myself.

DrL: If you refuse to acknowledge his loving need for you, then—if he's a decent man—when your youngest is eighteen, he'll be gone—and you'll have lots of time for yourself.

That relationship was going to hell.

Self-centeredness finds many faces. One couple almost had their marriage annulled only after a couple of weeks. Though they were both twenty-eight, she was stuck in her adolescence always wanting mommy and daddy's approval for everything. *"I didn't care too much about my husband's opinion on things. After realizing that my husband was very serious about the annulment, I finally placed my husband as the priority and finally opened up my eyes that he is not the enemy, but now my real, true family."*

Marilyn came to realize that too as her life was all about pleasing her difficult parents, she accommodated them and took her frustrations with that situation out on her husband. She still has familial issues, but she deals with them now as his wife, not their daughter.

Another typical self-centered motivation for tracking a marriage into hell is deciding that your spouse is boring. *"After 3 years of marriage,"* wrote Kris, *"I decided my husband was horribly boring and unromantic. We never did anything exciting, and I somehow felt as if MY happiness was HIS responsibility. I moved out and stayed with a friend and went out on a few dates. This was the life! This was exciting! And after all, as a child of the 70s flower children, I knew it was most important to do what makes you happy, right? Why shouldn't it be all about me-me-me?"*

It took Kris only a couple of weeks to realize how completely selfish she was being. *"All I had to do to save my marriage from the brink of disaster was to stop being an idiot. It's really that simple."*

The thing about bored people, as I mentioned in an earlier chapter, is that they are boring. Once Kris focused in on how wonderful her husband was, and how lucky she was that he was still open to her after her shenanigans, she spent her time making sure that he was well taken care of—never a dull moment after that!

Brian admitted that *"stopping my drug addiction really saved my marriage."* Taking responsibility for out-of-control, self-focused behavior without blaming your spouse for your actions is a tremendous boost to a marriage teetering over hell. Drinking, drugs, gambling, pornography, video games, and so forth, when compulsively done, are self-centered activities geared toward instant gratification and distraction from problems and feelings that need more constructive forms of attention.

A recent caller, twenty-eight years old, told me that she just finds it too impossible to be nice, loving, and sexual with her husband despite his wonderful nature. They've been married five years and have two little children. She told me she'd been in therapy since childhood concerning sexual abuse by a stepdad, and an unfortunate first marriage to an abusive guy.

DrL: How did all that therapy help you be able to love your husband?

Caller: Well, actually it didn't. I learned that I was a victim, that nothing was my fault, and that probably my husband earned my negative feelings toward him.

DrL: Brace yourself, my dear, for an alternative view. I think you are feeling so safe with this nice guy, that you feel free to be the perpetrator.

Caller: What????

DrL: Exactly. The tables are turned and now you have control and dominance and feel safe. However you're no longer in a situation against which you have to defend yourself. This is payback against the guys—your stepdad and first husband—who hurt you, but aimed at an innocent party AND your own potential happiness.

Don't you see that the first part of your life was taken up by predators and this, the second part of your life is also . . . except that the perp this time is YOU!

Caller: Whoa—I never thought about it this way, but I think you're right. What can I do?

DrL: Drop your guard, trust your husband, and love him up and have fun with him. No more fear—just more fun.

Caller: That sounds absolutely great. No therapist ever
told me anything positive I could use to be happy—it
is as if they all catered to my ugly history and not any
potential for a beautiful tomorrow.

There are some good therapists out there, if you're lucky
enough to find one. Mary wrote to me about what happened
a decade ago when her marriage was indeed on the brink of
divorce because of her husband's adultery.

> *"What saved it for me was that we entered into therapy with
> a counselor who thinks an awful lot like you do, Dr. Laura.
> Without excusing my husband's behavior, she repeatedly redi-
> rected my assessments from his behavior to mine. Meaning, every
> time I wanted to rehash what my husband had done to me, she
> forced me to examine how I had contributed to the problem.*
>
> *"Instead of entering into a fast food mentality of 'sit 'n
> bitch' every week, with fingers pointing at what the other party
> had done that was so egregious, we were constantly forced to
> examine our own behavior.*
>
> *"People go into couples' therapy with an agenda to change
> the other person. 'If only my husband would just do/not do this
> or that, then I'd be happy.' Imagine two people sitting in chairs
> across a room, each one waiting for the other one to change their
> behavior; each one waiting for the other one to lead!*
>
> *"Rather than allow us to marinate in our own disillusion-
> ment and bitterness with the other, we were directly to examine
> what needed to be changed about OURSELVES!"*

And that is why Mary and her husband are happily back
together again.

Abraham wrote about his marital problems, acknowledging

that his angry, critical behaviors were more about people in his past who hurt them, and not his wife, who got the brunt of it. *"Dr. Laura once said on the radio to a caller, 'Expect from your wife only what she can give you today. Don't expect her to make up for other people's abuse or shortcomings. She's your wife, not your mother.' "*

These days Abraham works hard on seeing her positive attributes and always considers her opinion. When he wants to criticize or point out some fault, he thinks long and hard about whether or not it is truly necessary to do so. If he decides that it is important, he thinks a few moments about exactly what he wants to say, lowers his tone, gets straight to the point, and points out that he is in no way trying to put her down. *"I always try to remember that I am not so high and mighty myself either."*

I usually remind listeners who feel some anger at their mate rising up within them to pair each critical thought or judgment with a positive or loving memory of them. It is too easy to do damage to a beloved when that tally sheet is momentarily out of balance. Always balance it in your mind before you speak.

It is also typical for people to just get too embroiled in their own importance with work, charity, children, family, or the problems of friends. These are ultimately all self-centered activities when they clearly preclude time, attention, affection, and respect for your spouse and family.

Personal ego gratification at the expense of family is a no-no.

COMMUNICATION

Mostly learn to "shut up." Just because it crosses your mind, don't assume it should come through your lips. Where did you ever get the notion that free speech meant you didn't have to consider appropriate restraint when dealing with the feelings of a beloved or the well-being of the entire family?

I realize that most discussions about communication have to do with actual "talking," but I'm of the opinion that more people need to learn to shut up than need to learn how to say something stupid or hurtful in a better way.

Certain things once said cannot be taken back. Too many spouses seem to imagine that they have some sort of protective immunity so that they can be cruel—with the excuse of hormones, bad day, need to vent—and there will be no real ongoing consequence. You're going to get only a few "get out of jail free" cards, and then the awe, respect, admiration, and love for you will start to wane.

Before you speak, think first about whether or not this will add to happiness and peace. Better still, cut your communication 15 percent, and fill the other 85 percent of the time with touching a hand, offering a cup of coffee, a neck rub, a hug, a sweet compliment, and so forth. Remember— TALK IS CHEAP and ACTIONS SPEAK LOUDER THAN WORDS . . . unless, of course, the words are mean or lies.

People just want to be treated with warmth, love, respect, and support. They don't want to hassle every detail of life. One quick way to bring your marriage back from the brink is NOT to talk it to death, but to instantaneously just start BEING NICE. You can't convince somebody you've changed . . . you've got to actually change. It might take them a while to believe and trust it, so don't do the "I tried it and it didn't work" schtick. If you want this marriage bad enough—EARN IT!

YOUR SPOUSE IS A SAINT

Some of you have seriously earned being dumped. The only thing that saves the day is that your spouse is a saint. Some of that sainthood might be part afraid to let go and be alone or even seemingly futile hope; maybe they just see more to you than you realize you have and are. Whatever it is, they give you another chance. DON'T BLOW IT!

Russ, a listener, wrote:

> "When my wife and I got married I was an angry young man with a chip on his shoulder and a bad temper. I grew up in a violent home. This June 19, 2006, will be our 35th anniversary and I thank God every day that she stayed with me and helped raise me.
>
> "My wife learned somehow, probably because of my explosive reaction, that challenging me in public back then was not a good thing and she was more effective in a private conversation with me. She was able to make her point, even though most of the time I was more concerned with winning the argument in my eyes than the actual point of the argument.
>
> "I was very immature and selfish probably the first 10 years of our marriage. I credit my wife and the Lord for what I am today (not that I think I am special now) and the great relationships we have with our kids, their spouses, and our grandchildren."

So what makes his wife a saint and not a patsy? It is interesting that Russ suggested himself that one of the typical mistakes women make is accepting poor behavior from their husbands, thinking it will get better. Ironically that is exactly what did happen for Russ. Why? Probably because his wife was not weak—she *didn't accept* his behavior, she dealt with it in a way which didn't cause the situation and his behavior to escalate. They had known each other since they were fourteen and sixteen; she had compassion for his family situation and how it impacted him—she was there to witness it. Her compassion, however, would probably not have stayed intact had he not demonstrated self-control at significant moments.

She made an investment, she took a risk, and her gamble paid off. It doesn't always. Although Russ pointed to that ten-year mark as the turning point for his behavioral changes, I bet it was more consistent and gradual—so she had reason to believe that her way of dealing with him worked.

Stefanie was prepared to leave her husband two years ago. They had been married seven years, and fought the whole time.

> *"The name-calling on both our parts was out of control. Having three small children and both working full-time (oppo-site shifts so one of us was always home with the kids) was stressing us both out. I also was always 'too tired' to have sex with him. I didn't take care of him. We hated each other.*
>
> *"I had an affair and my husband found out. Rather than kick me out like I deserved, he cried and said, 'You broke my heart.' This coming from the man I thought hated me!*
>
> *"We went to counseling and learned to stop the name-calling. My counselor must have been a Dr. Laura listener because I was told to be happy that my man always wanted to have sex with me and to give it to him whenever he wanted. After all, even if I was 'too tired,' wouldn't I enjoy it too? The counselor said that the fact that my husband still found me incredibly sexy and beautiful after seven years and three kids was wonderful, and that some women didn't have a husband like that.*
>
> *"I did nice things for my man. Two years after the affair, we get along better than ever. Whenever I make the mistake of turning him down for sex because I am 'too tired,' I stop for a minute, think about the past, put on a movie for the kids, and call him upstairs.*

"I am so lucky he stuck with me. I used to hate him, now I would literally give him my heart if he needed it. He is my man, the father of my children, and I thank God every day for him."

If your spouse shows any glimmer of cutting you some slack or supporting your better self—take it humbly, graciously, seriously, and lovingly. Give daily thanks to him/her in every way imaginable. Don't take advantage of a second chance; don't get all defensive and try to even up the score. Don't be stupid; do be grateful and take the opportunity to become a better human being, spouse, and parent. Become the person you'd be more proud to be with, feel safe with, and loved by.

IT'S THE SMALL THINGS, STUPID!

Most people get it into their heads that personal change and marital repair have to be huge, overwhelming issues. KISS: keep it simple, stupid! Or KISS: keep it small, stupid! Both concepts work. Heath wrote to me that he and his wife were pretty much finished. They did little as a team and when things got frustrating, Heath would lash out at her by saying mean things. He felt pretty much reduced to *"a walking paycheck with a penis attached. My job ground me down too. My wife didn't care about that, so long as the MONEY kept coming in and her health insurance was covered. We were finished."*

What turned things around was something very small. It started with the simple good deed of my wife bringing me a hot lunch during my break time at work. *"Such a small act paid such great dividends as the job didn't seem so life-draining nor did the workday seem as long. Sometimes she'd bring my dog to visit me as well, which really helped me keep things in perspective, that what I was doing was worth SOMETHING."*

What goes around comes around works for good things too. Heath started finding ways to help her at her workplace, like bringing her a rose or lunch. *"Ultimately, everything turned around. Marriage becomes less difficult when your partner helps you with your struggles. And the sex gets better as well. *wink wink*."*

KISS versus imagining you have to go through the hell of rehashing old hurts and angers. KISS versus thinking you have to wait eons for there to be good feelings back in the relationship. KISS versus believing that there is no hope. KISS . . . yeah, I do mean literally!

Chapter 6

Mother Laura's Marriage Tools

You all have heard the admonition, "If it ain't broke, don't fix it." Well, sometimes folks forget that when it is broke, they should do whatever it takes to fix it rather than give up and throw the marriage away, pull inside themselves, run to someone else for validation, or start attacking in order to look like the one in the right or the victim.

Admittedly there are times though that you might feel so emotionally distraught that it is hard to think of what you should and could do. Combine that with the fear of failure or rejection, and you may just emotionally run and hide.

Here are ten alternatives. Memorize them! Live them!

1. **There is no "I" in TEAM!** When your marriage is on the brink of divorce, when there is no communication and you're both miserable and figure you need to do something about it or cut it off then and there, it is time to . . . what? Well this is exactly why there is such a high divorce rate; most folks don't really know what to do at the moment that the feelings are so

high, or low, that you can't imagine anything good coming out of whatever you say or do.

As I mentioned earlier, Aaron, Moses's brother, healed a shattered relationship between two former best friends by meeting separately with each and telling them a special kind of lie. He told each that he had run into the other and heard nice things about them! Now what makes this a "special kind of lie" is that in truth, each *had* nice things to say about each other—for years! It's just that they hadn't said any of those things recently because they were damn angry about something or other. When each heard that the other said something nice about them, it brought back their own nice thoughts about each other. The next time they met in the street, they embraced instead of ignoring each other. There is a lesson here: when the going gets to feeling hopeless and way too ugly, it is time to remember the covenant and your earliest dreams and hope for the relationship. You are a team. Stop thinking only that you are sleeping with the enemy.

Instead of giving him/her a list of their failures, give your beloved a list of your points of appreciation and a list of the things you intend to do for them! That's right—for them! And this is true *even if* (the favorite phrase of many of my callers) you believe you are the victim here. Do it! It will remind your beloved that you are a team and that will be more motivating than forcing them to feel humiliated and beyond redemption.

2. **Down Memory Lane.** Tommy and Coral, listeners, had been just sharing the same house, leading sepa-

rate lives. Coral says she was praying for ages that she could love him again. Basically, however, they were like brother and sister. She is seventy-one, and he a young eighty-two. This was their second marriage (of fifteen years) as both had lost their first spouses.

One day while Coral, who didn't cook anymore, was making dinner for a sick neighbor. Her husband walked by and saw the stir-fry pan and said that he remembered that pan. " *'I fell in love with you when you cooked me dinner in it.' I said, 'Well, I fell in love with you while we were dancing and I don't cook anymore and we don't dance anymore, so I guess we both got gypped.' "*

One week later Tommy wrote "dancing" on Coral's "to do" list. They went dancing.

"Tommy is the most fantastic dancer and he has the cutest expressions on his face—it made me fall in love with him all over again. People tell us that we look like a couple of lovebirds. When we are being passionate, I say, 'Are old folks like us supposed to be having this much fun?!' Oh, and I also cook more.

"This has been the greatest miracle in my life. My prayer was answered beyond my wildest dreams. I always thought that Tommy should have someone who adored him. I never though that someone would be me."

Remember back to what made you "fall in love" and make that memory live today.

3. **Mutual Forgiveness.** Kimberly and her husband had the most wonderful, romantic courtship, engagement, wedding, honeymoon . . . but then nothing else

seemed to fall into place after their first year together. Loss of jobs, changed professions, unplanned and difficult pregnancies, having to drop out of college, a severe car accident, family deaths, financial problems, relocations . . . led to a lot of bad, hard feelings between them.

"When we came to our five-year anniversary nothing seemed right. That actual night [of their anniversary] we took our son to a sitter and ended up at home in the worst fight ever. We vented. There was screaming, things were broken, many tears and the word divorce was thrown out on the floor as the solution to our nightmare. However, almost as soon as we realized that it could happen, we verbalized to each other that this was not what we wanted.

"We then did something special that brought healing and the ability to press on. **We forgave each other. We agreed to let the past die and start over.** *We went from being on opposite sides of the room, to holding hands and praying together. My husband then led me to where we kept the copy of our vows. We had our own little ceremony. We recommitted and said our 'I dos' again. We hugged and kissed and then went and picked up our son. We went to bed that night in peace.*

"We were poor, there were no gifts or romantic getaways for our 5th anniversary; but I will remember it forever. It was an incredible night about true love and our decision to keep it happily ever after."

4. **Dump Your Prideful Ways.** Most of the time you both probably behave very badly when your beloved tells you how you've hurt them or gives you any criti-

cism at all. You probably don't take the time to really listen, instead you just get all defensive and attack back to try to make yourself look better—and it works the opposite way!

Just listen! By that I mean, listen without speaking—don't explain, excuse, or defend yourself. Just listen! Show respect for the state of mind, perspective, and feelings of your beloved. Keep your lip buttoned and just listen.

After you've heard it all, find some part from 1 percent to 99 percent of what she/he says that holds water and **own it!** Accept that you have failed or let someone down. Admit that you were insensitive, wrong . . . whatever. It is not constructive to try to prove that you are right and they are wrong. Even if you think you have a great explanation or excuse—they are feeling hurt; acknowledge your part in that.

If you **own it,** take responsibility, show true remorse, try to repair it, and clarify how it will not be repeated, then you have given your beloved a gift that will tsunami back with loving rewards.

5. **Ignore the Sometimes Not So Small Stuff.** Everybody has lousy parts of their personality—everybody. Jim wrote that he and his wife were able to avoid divorce by taking responsibility for their own actions and focusing on how to personally change rather than make the other change. Jim would get physically violent when angry; and what made him the most angry, was when his wife would curse at him and use her words to hurt him.

"I made myself accountable by writing a letter to my wife stating that if I ever physically hurt her again, I

would call the police on myself. I also learned how to direct my frustrations more constructively and if I was feeling like I was getting 'heated up,' that it was okay to go for a walk and cool off.

"My wife's main problem was that when she felt like she was getting mad, she would find any word or phrase that she knew would hurt me. I had a problem with taking things from the woman I love very personally. She would provoke with her words, hurt me, I'd get heated up and then things would escalate.

"Now, however, if she swears (and it is rare now) I ignore it and later, as she does now, I know she will come back and apologize for the swearing."

Yeah, I know your beloved can cut you deeper than anyone else has the power to do; that's because you love them and have your emotional well-being attached to their feelings about you. And you are hurt by the seeming rejection that their anger feels like. Nonetheless it is never useful to escalate a situation by reciprocating with your own bad behavior.

6. **You're the Genius! . . . No, Honey, YOU'RE the Genius!** Remember that you two will each have a different point of view about any situation. Try to remember that two heads can be much better than one if you show some respect for the other's head! You might learn something useful, and you just might come up with a better solution together than each of you separately.

Instead of fighting your beloved's perspective, make the huge effort to find something good about it. That way, your spouse feels heard and appreciated, instead of someone you consider stupid and useless.

Try this: next time you're in a so-called debate about something (money, kids, relatives), instead of trying to convince your spouse that you're right, make a big deal about some part of their point of view that you think is terrific! Watch how quickly s/he will suddenly find something of value in your perspective. This is loving negotiation.

Don't let it get personal. When you discuss problems, make sure you keep it to the issue, some perspective, an idea, a solution, a dilemma, whatever, but DO NOT let it get personal in an ugly way. Avoid the name-calling and bringing up of past mistakes, and so forth. Is it more important for you to have your way than to have a marriage of happiness and peace? If you blow any of this, just say you're sorry IMMEDIATELY and ask for forgiveness . . . then screw up less and less, okay?

7. **Nicer to Strangers.** It is amazing to me how many people treat absolute strangers with more courtesy, kindness, and sensitivity than their own spouses and families! Why is that? Because they know they can get away with it with family—they feel safe from rejection and abandonment. It is all about taking advantage of love and taking love for granted. Don't—you have too much to lose and the potential of too many people being hurt.

"We are married because we love and enjoy each other— so why not treat each other as friends first? We practiced kindness, restraint, complimenting, and most important, get-

ting those nagging thoughts (if they are important) into the open instead of brewing on them for hours or days on end and then ferociously erupting at some later time," wrote Marsha, who revealed that they were on the brink of divorce five years earlier.

You should actually be treating your spouse with infinitely more regard than a stranger due to your covenant, and the gratitude you should have that someone tolerates your nonsense and would mourn your passing. A stranger won't mourn your passing. Don't treat your spouse so poorly that they won't either!

8. **It Is a Far Greater Blessing to Give than Receive.**
Mostly when we've had a bad day or are just out of sorts, we *need, want, demand, expect.* Problem usually is that either we don't communicate any of this, that is, ask for hugs, a neck rub, kind words, and so forth, or when/if we get some caretaking, we are critical or rejecting of it, or don't let it help us at all and we stay in a crummy mood.

I have always found that coming out of yourself at these times, while difficult, is better medicine. Do an errand for her/him. Get your spouse a little gift surprise, write a cute and loving note—you get the idea. You will, I promise, feel better faster than waiting and wanting stuff to come your way.

Then if you still need a little TLC, ask specifically for it in a reasonable, humble way. And when you get it, make a fuss about how wonderful they are . . . even if it's a little off the mark or doesn't do the trick.

9. **Forget Rewriting History.** *"I realized that the years of resentment weren't going to disappear overnight,"* wrote

Lynette about her marriage. That is such an important point. So many people yearn for the pristine and won't "let it all go" or "get on with today" because they are still marinating in the crap.

Lynette knew that her husband wasn't spontaneously going to get her off the hook for the long-term errors of her ways. He wasn't going to one day soon just blurt out, "I forgive you! I am madly in love with you and I want to be with you forever! I will never leave you again!" Healing takes time and you can't take the temperature of a marriage every five minutes in order for you to feel safe, while forcing your spouse to feel something they're not up to yet.

Best thing you can do when you've messed up is DO THE RIGHT THING FROM THIS POINT ON . . . and pray for the best.

10. **Kings and Queens.** Tracy wrote that *"Ten years into our marriage I didn't feel unhappy, but I knew I couldn't say that I was happily married either. I went home to my Grandma's to 'think' for a week. Grandma sent me back to my husband after a few days saying, 'It's as simple as this: treat him like a king and he will treat you like a queen.'*

"We are now into our twenty-third year of marriage and I can say without a doubt, I am one happy queen."

Give him/her what they want and need (unless it's immoral or illegal) *even if* it is not your cup of tea. Assuming you married a reasonable, decent person this will be reciprocated—I promise.

Chapter 7

The Gift of the Magi

Abe Lincoln quipped that "Most people are as happy as they make up their minds to be." In life and in love there are definite attitudes and actions that make people happier: gratitude, optimism, forgiveness, self-healthcare, and speaking positively. Many people hang on to gloomy, negative, and angry states of mind out of pure habit, and habits are difficult to break; difficult, but not impossible.

One recent caller, married only a handful of years and with a small child, called to tell me that she's probably going to end the marriage because they fight about everything and say hurtful things to each other. I asked her to try an experiment: every time she wishes to lash out with her words she was supposed to *first* say *two* things utterly complimentary. If, after that, she still felt like saying something mean—then go for it!

It is a fact that what comes out of your mouth is what sits on your brain. The more you talk to or about your spouse in angry, ugly ways, the more angry and ugly you are to them and feel about them.

Some of you reading this are probably aghast! You probably

can't imagine generating so much self-control from within or getting over the feeling that you'd be letting them get away with something. Well, if your goal is to be happily married, can you afford not to learn self control? Do you really want to make the love of your life feel quite that bad when they've upset you? Do you want this ferociously angry exchange to be the last thing s/he remembers about this marriage as s/he goes to sleep at night?

Rachel, a listener, wrote that she has not gotten along well with her husband's family due to some bad behaviors on both their parts. I was impressed that she did admit that she had responsibility for the family's being upset. She didn't have to deal with them more than once every four or five years because they lived in a different state.

The current situation arose since her husband had an important event, and some of his family flew into town to be at this event. Rachel didn't want to go to the dinner.

> *". . . and I just kept thinking what you, Dr. Laura, would say if I had you sitting across from me and I was whining to you about how I did not like these people and how 'UNCOMFORTABLE' (I know you always make fun of uncomfortable being used as an excuse since it is a small issue) they made me and why I couldn't just stay at home while my husband went out to dinner with his family.*
>
> *"You would have said that they paid quite a bit of good money to come and see my husband and to be there for him on his big day, and they are his family and he wanted them there on his special day. You would say that a good wife would not do anything to make her husband's life harder and you would ask me if I wanted to be a good wife or a bad wife.*
>
> *"Then you would tell me, 'Smile and be polite.'*

"I made up my mind that I was going to be kind, pleasant, friendly, and polite, no matter what anyone else did at dinner last night.

"Well, I was—and imagine my surprise at how pleasant the evening was. I am not going to delude myself about certain unchangeable facts about these people that make my whole 'Walton's Mountain' fantasy impossible, but they've grown up some and so have I since the last time I saw them. It really was a nice dinner and I look forward to seeing them today . . . to my utter shock!"

As I mentioned in the Preface, this is the point of the Gift of the Magi: to have a lovely marriage, give what is most precious to you. In Rachel's case, she gave of her loving, kind self in spite of her fears and hurts. She did it for the sake of the man she loves. This behavior is called altruism. Married people who display frequent altruism toward their beloveds have happier marriages. Spouses who have this self-sacrificing "put the interest of the other before my own interests" mentality are happier, and more happily married.

Tiffany's husband was studying to be a minister, so money was tight. He had just found a used PlayStation on sale for $40. She knew he loved to relax with a video game in between reading nonstop for his two college degrees. They had a couple of small, unexpected expenses show up later that week, and her birthday was coming up. They didn't have money for him to buy her a birthday present, and she told him it was truly okay, and that he could get her something down the line when the finances eased up a bit.

He asked her what she would have wanted had they the money to get it; she said a body lotion and body spray set that cost about $20. He promised to get it for her when he could.

"The next day, I came home from work and the entire apartment was cleaned and vacuumed, candles were burning, and dinner was cooking on the stove. I asked him what the occasion was. He replied, 'Your birthday, honey! Now let me go get your present.'

"He came out with a gift bag with the lotion and body spray set in the fragrance I had wanted. I couldn't believe it, and asked, 'How did you get this? We have no money!'

"He replied, 'I pawned my PlayStation. I would rather you have a birthday present than for me to have a video game machine.' "

I guarantee you, folks, that as happy as it made her to receive, it made him happier to sacrifice for her. Altruism, self-sacrifice, makes people happy. It also makes them loved. In order to be loved, you must first love. Love is not about you or what you want, it's about giving love without conditions to somebody healthy and kind enough to do the same.

Annette and her husband recently celebrated their twentieth anniversary.

"And as we look around and see people struggle in their marriage, and then we look at each other and we ask, 'Why are things so good for us? We're either in complete denial or things are pretty dang good.'

"Yes, we've had many struggles: infertility, miscarriages, business bankruptcy, moving from our home of 18 years to a new state, moving a business, building a new one . . . but I can narrow down a great marriage to the banishment of two words from our vocabulary and marriage: they are EXPECT and DESERVE.

"Too often partners in a marriage have way too many unrea-

*sonable expectations. There is no room for 'high horses' in a marriage, and if we focus on what our **partner** deserves, magically we get everything we need."*

That is the Gift of the Magi.

THE GIFT OF BECOMING "ONE"

The covenant of marriage generally includes the proclamation that two lives have joined into one. I wish more married couples would spend time considering what that really means outside of joint income tax forms and community property laws. Your spouse is not supposed to be your sibling with whom you compete for attention, importance, or power. There is no beauty generated by those motivations.

Danielle wrote that for her birthday, she

"sat at the picnic table with all my kids and hubby of 33 years. She thought, 'This is the life!' Yes, we have had our struggles because we are human, yet here we are eating a dutch oven supper my husband cooked for us. We laughed at the past and giggle at the stupids we have all committed, but the most important thing we all realized was that WE ARE A UNIT—AND WE ARE THERE FOR EACH OTHER COME HELL OR HIGH WATER!

"I am sure we will do stupid human tricks from time to time, but I can look forward with confidence that MY TEAM that was formed by blood, sweat and tears will be there to get each other through the tough and good times.

"It has been worth the trip—believe me—and when all is said and done and we die, the only thing we can take with us is the relationships we've formed and the integrity of our souls.

*I did the right thing and spent the day celebrating with the ones
I love . . . unconditionally."*

Life can be quite complicated and difficult. It is a blessing
and a relief to not have to go it alone. Cherish that.

Linda wrote that she had overspent quite a bit on her credit
card, due to less household money coming in. Her husband's
business is in a low cash flow position, due to new product
development, and he had been worried, cranky, and distant for
months. She admitted to spending sneakily because she didn't
want to deal with him, and because she has been somewhat
ticked off about the distance.

But after hearing me on my radio program giving advice to
a woman who had also sneakily overspent about not working
with her husband as a *team,* but instead treating him virtually
like an annoying and potentially punitive parent, she felt guilty
enough to face the music.

*"I paid bills, took a deep breath, and went to him with the
numbers, statements, and credit card. I updated him on the
bills, apologized for spending and not telling him, told him I
had been wrong and a BRAT, and turned my credit card over
to him.*

*"Dr. Laura, I was stunned by his response! With tears in his
eyes, he took my hand, kissed me, and then he TALKED—for
an hour. He told me he felt useless for anything but writing
checks now that the kids are grown—and since he couldn't even
write checks with the money so low, he felt even worse. With
college, a wedding, and all the other expenses with three great
kids left to educate, he's worrying about retirement. And he
misses the kids so much he can hardly stand it.*

"So we made a plan to hike more, visit the grandchildren,

*and make whoopee!—all free activities. I assured him that I'm
very good at not spending money, and would run all purchases
by him.*

"We are closer than we have been in months."

Linda and her husband went from him & her to we & us,
dealing with life as a team—facing challenges and enjoying
triumphs as "one."

THE GIFT OF UNDERSTANDING AND COMPASSION

One of the more typical behaviors that hurts the "we" and
"team" concept, is the turning on each other when life throws
us a curveball.

Amy: I am my two kids' mom. I have five-month-old
  fraternal twins. I just don't know what to do with my
  husband. I am working part-time right now and he
  just lost his job. For a month he's been looking for a
  job and I don't know if I should just go back full-time
  to my work and let him stay home and take care of
  the children.

DrL: Well, whatever you need to do to survive for the
  time being you need to do. That's what marriage and
  families do. That's what a team is, and if that's the best
  decision for right now, then that it what it is. Stuff
  happens. What did he lose his job for?

Amy: He was on probation and he didn't pass.

DrL: And that was because . . . ?

Amy: He has a back injury.

DrL: Then he was not irresponsible.

Amy: Yeah, but sometimes I get mad at him.

DrL: It's not fair to get mad at him, Amy. You're going to have to control that. You can't take your discomfort with real life out on your man. It's no fault of his own that he lost this job, and in addition, his back hurts and he's got a ticked-off wife. Do you want to just put his head on the floor and dig your heel into it?

Amy: Not really.

DrL: You're supposed to be the one person he can be safe with. And if you're not that person—you lose the marriage even if you stay together.

Amy: Right, and I love him.

DrL: He feels bad enough. There he is, he can't take care of his woman and his two kids because he has a back injury.

Amy: Yeah, I know.

DrL: Okay? A little compassion here. Build up his ego and make him feel better somehow. Tell him what a wonderful job he's doing with the kids.

Amy: So do you think me working full-time and him staying home is okay? That's better than them going to day care, right?

DrL: You have to ask that question? Hired help, virtual strangers already watching over too many screaming kids or one's daddy? I don't know—which do you think is better?!

Dawn called my program very bent out of shape because her husband wants peace and quiet in the home after eight P.M. on weeknights. Dawn pulled the "isn't he controlling" card out of the deck. They have two married children, and an eight-year-old daughter. All he asked for is that weeknights, when he needs to unwind, get rest so he can function the next day, that family and friends not stay past eight P.M.

Dawn: I don't know if I'm being selfish or he's being kind of controlling.

DrL: I don't think there's anything controlling about that. I just love the way women in particular jump to "controlling" when a man just simply wants something like peace and quiet in his home during the week. I don't think you'd call yourself controlling for wanting company to stay till late!

Dawn: Okay, but the other thing I was going to ask you was, like in the mornings—I can't turn on the bedroom light or anything, so I always have to get my clothes out the night before and try not to make noise in the morning.

DrL: Because he needs to sleep?

Dawn: Yeah.

DrL: So what is bad about that? I'm that respectful to my husband too if I have to get up before him. It's a matter of respect, Dawn. When you love somebody

you try to accommodate them out of love and compassion—and respect.

That issue of not giving to a spouse because it is "giving in
to their control" is a very sad commentary on what ought to
be a no-brainer: accommodate your spouse, especially in the
areas of peace and happiness.

Carrie called about her husband's desire to change what
they agreed would be the name of their baby son, so that the
son can be the IV in the family; it's tradition. I asked her why
she was so against it.

Carrie: I guess it's an identity thing—like he's just as
much a part of me as he is a part of my husband—and
I felt I was kind of being controlled into doing it.

DrL: A man wants something and it's controlling. A
woman wants something and it is entitlement. I don't
have a lot of sympathy for your point of view. This
baby spent nine months in your body and gains sustenance from the milk of your breasts? How do we even
that up with your husband so that he feels the baby is
also a part of him?

It's a simple gift, Carrie, which doesn't make the
baby less yours, and it doesn't make him controlling.

Carrie: No, I would agree. But in my defense, he did say
during my pregnancy, "Whatever makes you happy."

DrL: Guys say that so their wives won't bitch at them and
not give them sex. They're also saying that to avoid a fight
and in the hope of ultimate altruism from their wives.

Carrie: Right. So what do I do now?

DrL: Why don't you give him the gift? Make the family happy that it is four generations now. That's kind of cute. You give him this gift, he's going to give you many gifts back.

Carrie: Yeah, you're probably right.

Understanding and compassion—great gifts.

THE GIFT OF PERSPECTIVE

One of the most loving and helpful gifts is that of having or giving of a new perspective on things. For example, Janet wrote that she and her husband were driving home from his family's Christmas celebrations. She and her husband were discussing the obvious inconsistencies in how he and his sister were raised; his sister being the darling "cannot do wrong" sibling who delighted in getting him in trouble, while his boyish misbehaviors were met with severe punishments, bordering on abusive beatings.

Her husband was continuing to bitterly recount the imbalance in his boyhood home and his resentment at his sister even after all of these years.

"I looked at my husband and simply reminded him, that he is one of the most compassionate, empathetic people I have ever met. He is kind, gentle, loving, and genuinely a good person. He is by far the best person I have ever known in my life. All those experiences, as horrible as they were,

*seem to have added up to make him the man I fell in love
with eleven years ago.*

*"I also reminded him that his sister is lonely, bitter, selfish,
and for the most part, a not nice person.*

*"My husband then realized, as did we both, thank God for
the imbalance. How awful it might have been if he had been
the spoiled favorite—and what kind of person would he have
turned into under that kind of upbringing; maybe he might have
been the narcissistic, unlovable, and unhappy sibling!"*

They had a good laugh over that, he felt a feeling with Janet
that he never got as a child: ultimate love, respect, admiration,
and appreciation—all the while realizing that his pampered sister had none of that. The bitter rivalry melted away, all due to
Janet's loving "perspective" check.

Janet could have just said, "You know—get over it already
and stop acting like a baby. I'm sick of hearing about your
lousy childhood. Grow up!" Instead, Janet gave him the
perspective he needed to let go of that pain. Perspective is
a gift.

Giving yourself perspective is yet another way to give your
spouse a gift. Amy wrote about her adjustments during the
first few weeks of motherhood. It was a time when getting a
newborn to sleep at night was quite a challenge. This particular
night their daughter wasn't fussy, but when Amy laid her in
the bassinet, she was wide awake and squirming. Ryan, Amy's
husband, came in to check on them, kissed and petted Eva's
forehead, and went back downstairs.

A bit later, Amy was still sitting by Eva, who was quiet, but
still wide awake. Ryan came in again, this time to fill up the
humidifier for Eva and Amy with fresh water.

"I wanted to say 'Stop coming in here!' because I was afraid the commotion of the door opening, him walking around, etc., would stir Eva again. But I bit my tongue, just glad that he was so helpful.

"After a while, Eva was still awake, but quiet, so I ran downstairs to quickly grab some water. I was dying to be able to sit next to Ryan on the couch for a few minutes, but I had to get back upstairs. So I gave him a quick hug around his neck, kissed him, and told him good night. THEN—and here's where Dr. Laura helped me—I almost said, 'And don't come into her room anymore!!!!—It'll just wake her up!' But I didn't. I didn't let my bitterness that I couldn't relax with him make me snap at him. I am so lucky that he is such an involved dad and that he loves her enough to check on her and give her one more kiss. So I didn't make any rude or snippy comments.

"Eva fell asleep so I crawled into bed and closed my eyes. Ryan came in. My first thought was 'Grrr! What do you want?' but I kept quiet. 'Sleeping?' he whispered. 'Yeah,' I answered. Then he hopped into bed with me and began making love to me! How nice that with all the above, he wanted his wife! It was so great! I'm SO glad I wasn't a bitch earlier. Thank you, Dr. Laura, for helping me to be a pleasant wife. It was you vs. the post-pregnancy hormones—and you (and I) won!"

It is all in how you **choose** to look at it, isn't it?

THE GIFT OF HEALTHY FOCUS

Many married men and women use a million excuses for not making sure that their relationships with their own moms and dads don't infect their marriages. They'll cater to their parents' unreasonable requests and whims, they'll spend an inordinate amount of emotional time and energy fretting over pouty, manipulative, threatening, difficult, and even mean parents— hoping uselessly that they can finally get parental love.

What I remind folks who call me from these situations is "It is a terrible thing that you do not accept and reconcile your destructive past and present issues with parents because you are so narrowly focused on your childlike needs to be perfectly parented, that you don't seem to be even aware of the damage you do your spouse and your children with your constant distressed state of mind!" That is most usually a revelation to them.

But not to Helene:

"Reading Bad Childhood Good Life *gave me the biggest boost of my life. I can't believe I've wasted so many years feeling sorry for myself because I have a cold, selfish mother. I put myself and my family through hell, trying harder and harder to please her, thinking that I could change her into the sweet, kind mother I'd always wished for. But of course she never changed and it only frustrated me to tears.*

"I used to obsess about this every day with my husband— poor guy. I'm so ashamed that I put him through that. But I'd been pitying myself and in the process I know I was driving my husband crazy. I'm so embarrassed. Honestly, if you hadn't written this book, I would no doubt still be crying about my mother day after boring day to my dear husband.

"You're absolutely right that I have a second chance at a happy family life with my own husband and children. And I'm so blessed that I picked a wonderful, caring husband and we have two great kids! So now I remember to count my blessings. I'd been feeding those 'poor me' thoughts for years—but now I finally get it."

Another source of extended family problems being allowed to negatively impact marriages is when some parent doesn't approve of or like your spouse, or refuses to acknowledge them or treat them with respect. Yes, you have to choose! You need to tell your difficult parent that the price of admission into your life is their respectful and polite treatment of your spouse. Without that—you're gone from their lives!

Give your spouse the gift of your loyalty, and your most healthy psychological self.

THE GIFT OF INTEREST

There is no way in the world that you can really "give a damn" about all your spouse's interests. I know that when and if the discussion gets to cars or sports, my brain clouds over. It probably is the same when I try to explain some technical sail racing technique I've learned, or how I found a new way to work stones in the necklaces I make for charity. Does this mean we're entitled to say "I don't care—shut up and leave me alone?" Well not if you love him/her—and not if you want to be happily married.

> *"Your book* The Proper Care and Feeding of Husbands *helped me to see how completely ONE-WAY I had become in my marriage. I went so far as to tell my husband that 'I didn't care about his job and to stop boring me with the details of his day.' Can you even imagine how he managed to come home every night and be decent to me? He did, but I always felt he wasn't giving ME enough.*
>
> *"Halfway through reading your book, I put it down and looked him right in the eye and told him that I was sorry. He works very hard every day to allow me to stay home and raise our children—and all I could do was tell him to shut up?*

"I told him I would always be there and there was nothing too trivial to discuss with me ever. Two days later, on Monday, I met him at the door with a giant kiss and sincerely asked him what his day was like and if there was anything I could do to help him unwind. After he got over the shock, he told me about his day—and listening wasn't hard after all. He then asked me if he could help me with anything. This was new for both of us, but terrific as well.

"Since then, I have made him a priority in my life, and the rewards have been immeasurable. My kids are even happier. I look forward every day to seeing my man walk through the door and he tells me he can't wait to get home!"

That's the power of the gift of showing/having interest—genuine interest is a form of caring; and you ain't a'gonna get some if you don't give some.

THE GIFT OF GRATITUDE

It is way too easy to get yourself all worked up about how you're not getting what you want, exactly the way you want it. Even if you're right, you're missing the bigger picture, and a sense of peace and happiness in your life and marriage.

Andie wrote that she used to think her husband was terribly UNromantic and it made her sad, disappointed, frustrated, and angry. Nothing has changed in terms of her husband's behaviors. But now, miraculously, she thinks he is the most incredibly romantic man and she is deliriously happy! How is that possible?

When they were dating, he brought her flowers only twice: once for her birthday, and another time to apologize for a silly argument. Since they married, she can count on flowers for all special holidays, as long as she goes with him to the supermarket to pick them up. She usually has to plan their activities on these special days as well, as he gets stressed and grumpy about the pressure.

So why is she so in love with him that she still gets butterflies when she hears his ring tone on her phone?

"Instead of bringing me flowers, he brought me two children. He gets up before the sun every morning and comes home after dark so that we can afford for our children to have their mommy home with them all day. He went to school for eight years to get a job that he doesn't particular like, so that we can afford to live somewhere that we really love. He takes our family to church every Sunday so that the children will grow up knowing that God loves them and that their daddy loves God. He compliments my cooking—even though I know that I am not a good cook. He tells me I'm beautiful, and means it, even though my body looks like I went through a taffy puller each time I gave birth. He takes Saturdays off so that we can spend the day together, even when he'd like to go out with the guys or get a few more hours in at the office. He tells people (and I've overheard him) that he loves me for staying home and doing the most important job: raising our kids. And the most romantic thing of all is that he has never, not one time, gone to bed without saying, 'I love you.' "

Young folks today need to learn from Angie what ROMANCE is really about—and it isn't the behavior in a Harlequin novel.

Jonathan's definition of romance is this description of his wife: *"She always makes me feel loved from the moment I walk in the door with a kiss and a hug. She helps me feel like the sexy man in her life."*

Big deal flowers and candy. Bigger deal that your beloved takes care of your soul and psyche.

THE GIFT OF AHA!

Scottie wrote an apology note about her regrets to her husband. She apologized for her misbehaviors toward him for so many years: rejecting his love, being extremely selfish and self-centered, and not putting their relationship first. Her letter was all the more touching because she wrote that it made her feel so terribly sad to remember how she'd hurt him and how sorry she was.

> *"I had a huge aha! moment. That 'aha!' was: all you ever wanted from me is LOVE. I was always attaching a mood of emotion to keep me away from that one thought . . . LOVE. Why didn't you know what I (!) needed; why didn't you say exactly what I(!) needed to hear; why, why why!? I realized that it isn't all about what I'm not getting, it's about what I'm giving that makes the difference. I want to express my love to you fully. I am not looking for anything in return (anymore) . . . seriously, I long for your touch and will make sure you never feel rejected again. It is my pleasure to be your spouse and your lover."*

An aha! moment is one in which you own up in your own mind and heart to your failures, errors, and hurtful behaviors toward the one who should be your most cherished—and then you admit it to your beloved and make changes. It is not good enough to "try" to make changes because that attitude gives you a built-in excuse for any small failure to release you from your obligation to change. The gift of changing requires you to persevere in your changes in spite of any personal discomfort or disappointment in your beloved's instantaneous reaction; it may take some time for him/her to feel trusting and open again to you. You have to have the compassion and fortitude to proceed forward based on what is right, not what gets immediate applause.

Jake, another listener, wrote that he decided to try something he heard me talking about on my radio program to another caller who was having issues with feeling "good" enough to be nice. I suggested that no matter the mood, say something nice. Period. Just do it. So Jake wrote that *"Well, I am learning from listening to you . . . if I can communicate, say something positive like wishing them well with something, that it truly helps 'my spirit' and there is nourishment and freedom in this. A seemingly simple mindset and these little gestures of kindness toward someone else creates freedom and a better life for me too!"*

Jake's aha! was that he can generate a good feeling inside himself—freeing himself up from a darker moodiness and freeing up a relationship from tension—simply by saying something nice.

Whether it's that you have a drinking problem, you allow your parents and family to be too intrusive into your lives, you exhaust yourself so that you have nothing to give to your spouse, you allow your moods to dictate whether or not you are loving, you're too focused in on money, power, and acquisition as the main point of your existence, you keep trying to prove to your spouse that you are smarter, better, stronger, or that you've let your fears and hurts from your past take up residence in your marriage—it's time for you to have an aha! moment.

Admit your weaknesses and wrongs to yourself and to your spouse. Get professional and spiritual guidance to help you morph into your better self with options for a deeper happiness. You know, most of you rue this thought because you believe that if you show your weaknesses and admit your wrongs that you will be disdained and punished forever. Well, that's true only if you're married to a horrible jerk. Most of you are married to decent folks who will be touched beyond imagination by your gift of the aha! You will gain the love and respect you've yearned for and have gone after the wrong way!

Forget pathological or false pride. Remember only the gift of love.

Another source of an aha! moment is anytime you learn. Carly's fiancé picked her up at home and told her they had a special outing. Their first stop was a florist's shop where he picked up six yellow roses. He came back to the car and instead of handing the flowers to her he put them in the backseat. She was perplexed and curious.

They drove across town and he stopped at a retirement/ assisted living home. They got out of the car and went to the front desk where he introduced himself and the attendant, obviously aware of their visit in advance, took them down a long hallway where they were shown a door, and told, "They are expecting you."

"My fiancé knocked on the door, which was answered by a lovely older woman who invited us into her home and introduced her husband. I had never met these people but smiled and sat down in her living room. Then my fiancé said, 'Tell us your secrets. . . .'

"I came to learn that he had called and asked if there were couples that were married longer than 50 years and could we come speak with them. The assisted living home found us 6 couples married between 50–65 years for us to speak to—or

rather, to speak to us. They each shared with us their 'secrets' to a long marriage and their advice and best wishes for us. The yellow roses were for each of the women. It was an amazing evening where I learned a lot from 6 couples who had 'been there.' "

On the way back from meeting these couples, her fiancé apologized for not getting her a rose too. She took his hand, and with tears running down my cheeks, thanked him for the beauty that those six yellow roses brought into my life that no single rose given to her could have had.

"I remember the advice from those wonderful couples and, on days when he is driving me crazy (as I'm sure there are many when I do the same for him), I remember those 6 roses and the wonderful gift he gave me before we were married so that we can share our 'secrets' in another 45 years."

There are aha! moments all around you. Open your eyes, ears, mind, and heart to them. Perpetual learning of how to be more caring and loving is a great gift; better than any flower or trinket.

THE GIFT OF DEEP ACKNOWLEDGMENT

"Thank you so very much, Dr. Laura, for encouraging us female types to be feminine, not feminists. I am so lucky to have a husband who adores me, even after 17 years! He tells me often how much he loves me, but the best way to tell me happened the other day.

"He recently got a new computer for himself and went through all the process of installing software, setup up e-mail

accounts, etc. A few days afterward he sent me an e-mail and I noticed something so sweet it made me cry. You see, he listed me in his contacts folder as 'Shannon, the greatest wife ever.'

   "How wonderful to be cherished so much—he did that only for himself, but it meant so much to me. Makes me want to be an even better woman for him."

Obviously he had Shannon on his mind. Her husband probably didn't even realize that she'd see her address listing. Finding these things out accidentally is very touching because any sense of "s/he's just being nice out of habit or obligation" . . . or "s/he wants something," is totally eliminated!

Nonetheless deep acknowledgments of admiration are a blessing of incredible proportion! By deep I mean way more profound than the usual platitudes already written in a Hallmark card.

The following fifty-seventh birthday note from a loving husband to a loving wife ought to be a guide for you to come up with your own for your beloved. It is not enough to say "I love you"; it is a far, far better thing to describe "why."

   "Happy 57th birthday. I have been thinking about this past year, and decided I should share with you some of the things that you do to make our marriage and life together such a wonderful and thriving relationship. This is not a complete list, but these things are certainly among the most impressionable and important ones.

   1. Scrapbooking—you are at your best when creating, designing, and putting together the material that shows and describes the great family experiences we have.

2. *Home and yard care—this is an unending and demanding job that you have done for years. You really have made our yard a Garden of Eden.*

3. *Health and nutrition—you are one of the most disciplined people I know for planning and controlling your eating and exercise. You fight one of life's greatest battles with rare conviction and personal self-control.*

4. *Curiosity and interest in learning—I love your unending interest in people, places, and things. It's fun to see how much enjoyment you get from reading newspapers, magazines, and books. I relish in your thinking about things and what they mean.*

5. *Grandmother—what a delight it is to see how much your grandchildren crave you and your attention. Their affection and love is well earned.*

6. *Friend—you are so kind to those who really need friends. You spend hours listening and sharing thoughts and feelings with those most in need.*

7. *Great meals—I can't tell you how much I appreciate having regular meals that are healthy, timely, tasty, and well prepared. It has helped me to maintain good health and I enjoy and look forward to them.*

8. *Religious class—you have a great spiritual depth that you cultivate and grow weekly.*

9. *Home—you have put your talented and creative touch on our home and furnishings and made it so comfortable that I would rather be here than anywhere else!*

10. *Intimate friend and companion—I appreciate your love and affection, your companionship and attention. Thanks for making me the center of your life and focus of all you do.*

"Thanks for a great year. I know there are many more to come and life will only get better. I give you a world of thanks for your love and dedication to me and our family. All of my love and all of my kisses!"

When was the last time you truly and deeply assessed the beauty and the blessing of your spouse? When was the last time you truly and deeply assessed yourself to see if you were earning your spouse's love, admiration, awe, and respect?

THE GIFT OF ALCHEMY

Alchemy refers to the pseudoscience of turning base metal into precious metal. While that is an impossibility, it is quite within your capacity to turn an ugly situation into a beautiful one.

Chris (twenty-eight) and Rachel (twenty-five) called my program after being married for only a year. Chris said, "Well, basically we wondered . . . we have our occasional disagreements. I tend to take them in stride and get over them pretty quick. Rachel tends to get . . . she's pretty sensitive and tends to think maybe there's something wrong with us. I wonder what advice you had for couples on engaging in what amount of disagreements and arguments are okay versus what's too much?"

This is a typical scenario for young people in new relationships. The shock of everything not being delightfully perfect all the time, and the worry that one won't be liked when warts show, and inexperience in thinking as "one" usually causes these rifts.

I suggested that "When tensions first rise, you have to ask yourself a question really fast, 'Did I make a mistake and marry a bad person?' Because if that is what you believe, get out fast. If that is what you know to be not true then ask yourself what is the point of being so ferociously hostile and angry at each other? If you didn't make a mistake in the choice of a spouse, and you really believe that the other person truly lives concerned about your welfare and has the best intentions toward you and has your feelings and your very life in their heart—then there is no point in being so ferociously defensive, hostile, manipulative about hurt feelings, or apocalyptic about a little spat. At the time you are the most angry, the most resentful, the most irritated—do something nice for the other person and something magical happens."

Turning an ugly moment into a beautiful one can happen subtly, simply, and lovingly. Just say, "You know, I'm feeling so angry, hurt, upset that I'm confused. I do know that I love you, you're wonderful and I want us to be calm and comfortable with each other ten minutes from now. I want you to be happy and to be happy with me. How can I give that to you?"

There it will be: dirt into bliss.

Laura, another listener, wrote to me that her husband is a great man who takes good care of her, but that his parents are not very pleasant to be around. Since they live but an hour away, they are invited over all the time, and her husband didn't see a problem with going to 90 percent of these events, she was starting to feel drained. Whenever she said she didn't want to go to see his family, her husband would take it personally. She was alternating between feeling bad for him and angry with his family.

After listening to my program a while she decided to put some of my principles into play.

"I chose as my 'love attack plan' to try to have Sunday afternoons and evenings by ourselves instead of with his family. In my head, we would still do birthday parties, occasional

Friday night games and pizza—but I wanted Sundays with my husband.

"So one day after church, we came home, I put a pork roast into the Crock-Pot (his favorite dinner) and I put on something a little 'more comfortable ☺.' I asked him sweetly if we could please ignore phone calls and any visits for a few hours. He agreed. I then asked him if I could have a back rub in the bedroom, and to see what else would happen ☺. He sprinted into our room, lit some candles, and gave me a 15 minute back rub and we continued to share an intimate afternoon. We then had a yummy dinner and watched a movie together. We have continued that Sunday tradition for several months now. A few weeks ago, I asked my husband if he wanted to go up on Sunday night for a dinner at his parents' because we hadn't been there in such a long time. He gave me a big hug and said, 'Thanks, honey, but I LIKE OUR SUNDAYS more than their Sundays.'

"Pulling my act together by caring for him allowed me to have the power more than any nagging, anger, or resentment had in our past!"

A great form of alchemy is to, in the immortal words of Vito Corleone, "I'll make them an offer they can't refuse." The best offer is love and attention.

THE GIFT OF ... YOURSELF

One particular call to my radio program generated a tremendous number of follow-up letters from listeners.

Jennifer: I'm calling because I'm married to an accountant so I'm more or less alone for the next month and a half (tax season). I had been planning for several months to come up with my kids to visit my parents during the month of March for a few weeks. And my husband knew about this, my parents knew about this—it was preplanned. My husband called last night to let me know that his work expects him to go to a social obligation on Tuesday and to bring his wife and I don't feel that it's fair for me to cancel my trip and drive down there.

DrL: You are already at your folks' home?

Jennifer: Yes.

DrL: And you've got three little kids?

Jennifer: Yes.

DrL: Let me give you another perspective on this. He's going to be busting his back for a month and a half. It's certainly nice to come home to have a warm wife and a warm bed and be able to smooch the faces of your sleeping children during this horribly difficult time of a month and a half. I think you looked at it as, "Well, I'm not getting attention anyway, I might as well not be here."

You didn't look at it as a wife.

Jennifer (sighing)*:* Yeah . . . But he did agree!

DrL: Oh husbands will agree to anything we want just to keep us happy and having sex with them. You know that. You know that he agrees to all sorts of things just to make sure that you're okay with him and he doesn't get punished. Men with wives are like boys with mothers. So don't tell me he agreed with it as the rationale for not acting like a wife. As a wife, you might think to yourself, "Well, you know what—he has just no time for anything and it would be nice if when he walked in the house there were food and warm bodies.

Jennifer: Even though he's working eighteen hours a day?

DrL: Especially when he's working eighteen hours a day. He's not out eighteen hours at a bar, he's working to support you and three kids.

Jennifer: Yes he is. He works very hard and does a great job of it.

DrL: Right, and frankly we could look at it the other way—that you abandoned him.

Jennifer: Oh, ouch!

DrL: If I were you—I'd go home and take care of my man. He misses you, he misses the kids.

Jennifer: Okay, I'll do it. I'll go home then.

Several days later I received a follow up e-mail from Jennifer:

"I called you on Monday about my obligation to my husband while I was on vacation. I wanted to know if I was 'obligated' to drive eight hours home to attend a social function with him for his work. You told me that I was not obligated, but that perhaps I wasn't thinking of this as a wife should.

"When I arrived home last night, he had music and a gourmet dinner waiting for me. And after the kids were in bed, there

was other entertainment . . . Dr. Laura, you have no idea how AMAZING my husband is. Thank you for helping me to remember."

Take a note, Jennifer, "YOU ARE AMAZING TOO!"

As you might imagine, I get a lot of questions from spouses of military, police, and firemen about how to handle their stress. Saralee, one of my listeners, is married to a marine deployed to Iraq. She started getting really frustrated looking at all the work she has to do around the home by herself. She started crying and thinking about how she would love to tell her husband how she hates doing all this yard work.

> *"I wouldn't because there you are on my shoulder telling me how I married a warrior. I have even passed on your advice to other military wives. Then, in the midst of my tears, there you were again today telling a wife that a warrior needs a woman with grit.*
>
> *"I made up my mind that I will not even think about telling my marine about what a bad day I'm having pulling weeds and doing other dirty things. After all, I am positive he would rather be here doing this than dodging IEDs.*
>
> *"I am a proud wife of a U.S. Marine who has a woman at home who wears the crown that says GRIT. I will make him proud for marrying me too. HOORAH!"*

The Proper Care and Feeding of a Marriage is to GIVE, GIVE, and GIVE some more—of your best self.

Epilogue

"My husband stormed into the house the other day, as angry as could be from a frustrating day of melting under the Arizona sun and dealing with incompetent subcontractors. He paced and fumed and poured his frustration out on me. He also made several comments about me, the house, clean laundry or the lack of, and so forth. After a few hours of this, I began to feel very defensive and fought the temptation to lash back at him. I tried to remind myself that it was the anger speaking—not the man—and I did my best to support and love him.

"Yesterday evening, it was I who was depressed, angry, and volatile. My husband came home, took one look at my face, and probably decided that running for it was a good idea. But instead, he gave me a kiss and marched straight for the kitchen. He plowed into the dirty dishes, made an amazing steak dinner for us, and watched our 9-month-old daughter while I hid in the bedroom and ate chocolate chip cookies.

"When the baby was in bed, my husband put his arms around me, told me that I was his Ishah (Hebrew for woman), and that he would carry me when I couldn't walk on my own. I collapsed in tears, and he just hugged me until I could speak

intelligently again. He apologized for his behavior the other day, and said that my gentleness with his anger helped him to calm down.

"We're a team and we cherish each other."

Sincerely, Christine.

For me, that says it all. Now it's your turn.

BOOKS BY DR. LAURA SCHLESSINGER

THE PROPER CARE & FEEDING OF MARRIAGE

ISBN 978-0-06-114284-0 (hc) • ISBN 978-0-06-114282-6 (pb)
ISBN 978-0-06-123399-9 (uab CD) • ISBN 978-0-06-122711-0 (CD)

In this *New York Times* bestseller, Dr. Laura forces married partners to take a hard look at themselves and each other, and reveals how to bring marriage back from the brink of disaster.

BAD CHILDHOOD—GOOD LIFE
How to Blossom and Thrive in Spite of an Unhappy Childhood

ISBN 978-0-06-057786-5 (hc) • ISBN 978-0-06-057787-2 (pb)
ISBN 978-0-06-085288-7 (CD)

In this important book, Dr. Laura Schlessinger shows men and women that they can have a Good Life no matter how bad their childhood.

THE PROPER CARE & FEEDING OF HUSBANDS

ISBN 978-0-06-052061-8 (hc) • ISBN 978-0-06-052062-5 (pb)
ISBN 978-0-06-056614-2 (cassette) • ISBN 978-0-06-056675-3 (CD)

Dr. Laura urgently reminds women that to take proper care of their husbands is to ensure themselves the happiness and satisfaction they yearn for in marriage.

WOMAN POWER
Transform Your Man, Your Marriage, Your Life

ISBN 978-0-06-075323-8 (pb)

A companion to Dr. Laura's bestselling *Proper Care & Feeding of Husbands*, *Woman Power* is filled with new information about the special power women have to transform their husbands, their marriages, and their lives.

TEN STUPID THINGS WOMEN DO TO MESS UP THEIR LIVES

ISBN 978-0-06-097649-1 (pb) • ISBN 978-0-694-51513-4 (cassette)

Using real-life examples, Dr. Laura teaches women how to take responsibility for personal problems and discover their potential for growth and joy.

TEN STUPID THINGS MEN DO TO MESS UP THEIR LIVES

ISBN 978-0-06-092944-2 (pb)

Dr. Laura tells men how to get their acts together and take control of their lives and their destinies— how to truly become men.

STUPID THINGS PARENTS DO TO MESS UP THEIR KIDS

ISBN 978-0-06-093379-1 (pb)

Dr. Laura marshals compelling evidence of the widespread neglect of America's children and convincingly condemns the numerous rationalizations to excuse it.

TEN STUPID THINGS COUPLES DO TO MESS UP THEIR RELATIONSHIPS

ISBN 978-0-06-051260-6 (pb)
ISBN 978-0-06-000055-4 (cassette) • ISBN 978-0-06-000058-5 (CD)

An invaluable guide for those struggling to find the right mate or to escape a bad relationship.

HOW COULD YOU DO THAT?!
The Abdication of Character, Courage, and Conscience

ISBN 978-0-06-092806-3 (pb) • ISBN 978-0-694-51651-3 (cassette)

In her lively, pull-no-punches style, Dr. Laura presents a workable moral philosophy based on personal responsibility and the true happiness of the moral high ground.

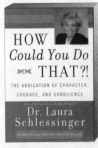

THE TEN COMMANDMENTS
The Significance of God's Laws in Everyday Life
with Rabbi Stewart Vogel

ISBN 978-0-06-092996-1 (pb) • ISBN 978-0-694-51955-2 (cassette)

Dr. Laura shows us how adhering to the higher ideals and consistent morality found in the Commandments can create a life of greater purpose, integrity, and value.